# SAN JUAN DE LA CRUZ
## by
## BERNARD GICOVATE

San Juan de la Cruz (Saint John of the Cross) is considered the greatest poet and mystic writer of the Spanish language. For over three centuries now he has been known and revered in the Western World as a profound religious thinker and as a poet of unequalled perfection in the utterance of divine love. Numerous translations have tried unsuccessfully to render the emotion and beauty of his verse into other languages. This study gives an introduction to the historical events of his times and explains the thought of Saint John of the Cross in the light of what is known about his life. After a survey of biographical facts and a summary of his thought and doctrine, this study presents an analysis of his poetry, its major themes, its structure, and its technique. Through explanation of lines and accurate, literal translation — printed always alongside the original Spanish — this study brings to the reader of English all the emotional richness of the poetry of Saint John of the Cross and makes his reading of the original easier and more rewarding.

*TWAYNE'S WORLD AUTHORS SERIES*

*A Survey of the World's Literature*

Sylvia E. Bowman, Indiana University
GENERAL EDITOR

# SPAIN

Gerald E. Wade, Vanderbilt University
EDITOR

## San Juan de la Cruz
(Saint John of the Cross)

*(TWAS 141)*

# TWAYNE'S WORLD AUTHORS SERIES (TWAS)

*The purpose of TWAS is to survey the major writers—novelists, dramatists, historians, poets, philosophers, and critics—of the nations of the world. Among the national literatures covered are those of Australia, Canada, China, Eastern Europe, France, Germany, Greece, India, Italy, Japan, Latin America, New Zealand, Poland, Russia, Scandinavia, Spain, and the African nations, as well as Hebrew, Yiddish, and Latin Classical literatures. This survey is complemented by Twayne's United States Authors Series and English Authors Series.*

*The intent of each volume in these series is to present a critical-analytical study of the works of the writer; to include biographical and historical material that may be necessary for understanding, appreciation, and critical appraisal of the writer; and to present all material in clear, concise English—but not to vitiate the scholarly content of the work by doing so.*

# San Juan de la Cruz

## (Saint John of the Cross)

By BERNARD GICOVATE

*Stanford University*

Twayne Publishers, Inc.   ::   New York

Library of Congress Catalog Card Number: 71-120481

## ABOUT THE AUTHOR

Bernard Gicovate is Chairman of the Department of Spanish and Portuguese and Professor of Spanish at Stanford University. He holds a B.A. degree from Bowdoin College, an M.A. degree from the University of North Carolina and doctorates from the University of Buenos Aires and Harvard University. He has received a Ford Faculty Fellowship, a grant from the American Council of Learned Societies and other awards for postdoctoral research at Columbia University, El Colegio de México, and La Sorbonne. He has taught at Tulane University, the University of California, and other American colleges and universities. His publications include *Julio Herrera y Reissig and the Symbolists* (Berkeley, 1957: University of California Press) ; *La poesía de Juan Ramón Jiménez. Ensayo de exégesis* (Puerto Rico, 1959: Asomante) ; *Conceptos fundamentales de literatura comparada. Iniciación del modernismo* (Puerto Rico, 1962: Asomante) ; and *Ensayos sobre poesía hispánica. Del modernismo a la vanguardia* (Mexico, 1967: Studium) . He is contributing editor for the "Poetry Section" of the *Handbook of Latin American Studies* published by the Library of Congress and is the author of numerous articles and reviews published in learned journals in the United States and abroad.

# *Preface*

In this introduction to the life and writings of San Juan de la Cruz (Saint John of the Cross), I have not tried to add more learning to the complex knowledge of history stored in our libraries. I have only tried to bring some understanding of the achievements of Saint John to those who have had little or no acquaintance with him and his writings. There is certainly no attempt to discover or even in any major way to synthesize previous knowledge in the following pages. My major desire has been to bring a few well-known Spanish poems to the attention of those who might otherwise find no occasion to study them.

The joyous sounds of Saint John's poetry belong definitely to his own language, and no translation can really reproduce them. Explanations are even less effective. Yet I have had to resort to both explanation and translation. If a glimmer of the grandeur of the original can still cast a spell on the reader, he may feel inclined to read the poetry of Saint John of the Cross in Spanish. The fragments in the original are quoted to satisfy this desire and in the hope that the reader will feel compelled to study the poems anew or for the first time. In either case, I hope that the explanatory introduction offered in these pages will not dampen the pleasures of discovery: perhaps it may induce them or make them more complete. My translations of several poems to be found at the end of the book are offered only as an aid in following the Spanish original. They try to be more accurate than the literary translations usually published. Since a critical text has not been established, I have overlooked many problems of detail and tried only to present a cogent English version without any artistic claim and as literal as possible, as far as the meaning of the original can be ascertained and translated.

An introductory chapter deals with the historical background and gives a sketch of the literature that preceded the writings of the great mystic poets of the sixteenth century. Obviously the few pages of the chapter can only attempt to give to those unacquainted with the literature and history of Spain a glimpse of the varied events and of the many problems of its past. They can only list the titles to be read and enjoyed some day. On the other hand, for those well acquainted with this background, the pages of this chapter might be just a rapid review to be glossed over with condescension. Chapters Two, Three, and Four relate the life of Saint John as a necessary prologue to the study of his doctrine in Chapter Five and of his poetry in Chapter Six.

In the laborious process of reworking what is known about Saint John and what speculation can add to knowledge, many sources have been consulted and used. The help of critics and historians is acknowledged in notes and in the bibliography. Nonetheless, I am sure I have forgotten many a debt. The assistance of Miss Virginia Higginbotham, Miss Sharon C. Philbrick, and Miss Sharon J. Swinyard in the preparation of the manuscript has been much more than mechanical. It began with the discussion of a vague possibility and continued through note-taking up to the last-minute correction of printer's proof. If the end result seems rather slight, the reasons must be sought in the difficulties of the subject or in the author's failure to utilize his material.

# Contents

# Chronology

1529 Gonzalo de Yepes marries Catalina Alvarez.
1542 June 24: Birth of Juan (John) de Yepes in Fontiveros, province of Avila.
1543 Publication of the works of Boscán and Garcilaso.
1545 First meeting of the Council of Trent.
1546 Death of Luther.
1547 Birth of Cervantes.
1548 Death of John's father, Gonzalo de Yepes.
1552- John's mother settles in Medina del Campo.
1554
1555 Charles V abdicates the throne of Spain.
1556 Philip II becomes King of Spain.
1558- John working in hospital in Medina and enrolled in
1563 Jesuit College.
1560 Group assembled in Saint Theresa's cell propose the foundation of a monastery of an eremitical type.
1562 Birth of Lope de Vega. Saint Theresa founds convent of Discalced Carmelite Nuns of the Primitive Rule of Saint Joseph at Avila.
1563 John receives habit at Carmelite House in Medina—takes name of Fray Juan de Santo Matía (Friar John of Saint Matthias).
1564- Attends the University of Salamanca—School of Arts.
1567
1565 *Life* of Saint Theresa.
1567 Friar John ordained priest. Meeting of Saint Theresa and John of Saint Matthias.
1567- John at the University of Salamanca, taking theological
1568 courses; appointed as prefect of studies while still a student.
1568 Appointed subprior and novice master of the first mon-

astery of Discalced Carmelites at Duruelo; changes name to Fray Juan de la Cruz (Friar John of the Cross).

Convents established at Duruelo, Malagón, Valladolid.

1569  Convents established at Toledo and Pastrana.

1570  Named Rector, Alcalá de Henares. Convent established, Alcalá de Henares.

1571  Battle of Lepanto.

1572  Confessor at Convent of the Incarnation.

1573  El Greco arrives in Spain.

1575  Reform group involved in conflict with Order over jurisdictional rights and censured by general chapter; Theresa humiliated.

1577  John imprisoned in Toledo.

1578  Escape from prison.

1578-   Writes *Subida del Monte Carmelo (Ascent of Mount*
1583  *Carmel).*

1580  Incorporation of Portugal and Spain.

1582  El Greco paints *Burial of Count of Orgaz.* Death of Luis de Granada. October 4: death of Saint Theresa.

1584  *Cántico espiritual (Spiritual Canticle). Llama de amor viva (Living Flame of Love).*

1588  Elected major definitor, thus becoming member of Reform's new governing body, headed by Father Doria. Defeat of the Spanish Armada.

1591  December 14: John dies in Ubeda, Andalusia.

1592  Body transferred to Segovia.

1618  First publication of some of Saint John's works in Alcalá de Henares.

1675  January 25: Beatification by Clement X.

1675  May 21: Translation of his body.

1726  December 27: Canonization by Benedict XIII.

1926  August 24: Declared a Doctor of the Church by Pius XI.

# CHAPTER 1

# *Introduction*

WHILE San Juan de la Cruz (Saint John of the Cross) is for us a poet whose religious experiences guided his thought, for his contemporaries he was a man of faith who wrote poetry. His task, as he saw it, was the instruction of young aspirants in the road to contemplation. If we view his experience in the light of history, he is the product of a religious crisis that made faith the central problem of European life of the sixteenth century. If we view history in the light of his experience, Saint John is the guide of great poets in his language and abroad and, at the same time, one of the founders and organizers of a religious Order which has been a major force in the Catholic Church. Even more important, the thought of Saint John has become part of a larger body of knowledge and speculation—a discipline called mystic theology.

Each of the many possible ways of studying Saint John's writings is equally valid and equally complete. But the only one which is real for us today, beyond the arguments of historical scholarship, is the road to an understanding of his poetry. His experience and his doctrine can be questioned; his poetry must be read. For an enlightened reading of his poetry we need, however, a previous knowledge of his experience and his doctrine and of the milieu in which his beliefs were nurtured.

It was Saint John's experience, not his poetry, that won him canonization in the Catholic Church. His poetry made this experience available to others, it is true, but it was never documentary evidence of spiritual attainments. In approaching the writings of a saint, then, the temptation to read his poetry as part of his saintliness is great. Such a reading would add nothing to Saint John's validity within his Church and would not be conducive to an understanding of his poetry. The opposite temptation is equally dangerous. His poetry could be read simply as a lyrical utterance of a person in love, without paying any attention to the intentions of the author. In this case, the complexity of Saint John's thought would be lost to the reader.

His poetry must be studied as an activity of the intellect, and the unbeliever must view it in the light of what Saint John himself believed about his own experience. Otherwise he may not understand even the literal meaning of his words.

Mystic experience, the communion of the mind with any divinity in which it believes, has been and continues to be part of the varied possibilities of man's imagination. In the sixteenth century, this experience was central in the life of the priests and nuns of Spain. Obviously, not everybody in orders attained or even aspired to the accomplishment of ecstasy. Yet the difference between their times and ours can be clearly seen if we reflect that the few who claimed this attainment were listened to and  reviled or glorified according to the whims of fate.

In all ages there have been men who have tried to reach perfection in the understanding of the Creator and Creation. They have believed that they could attain ecstasy and overcome the painful doubts of reason or ignorance. In Spain in the sixteenth century, this attempt was not sporadic and accidental, but codified and widespread. The people who claimed this experience were often highly articulate exponents of an eager humanistic culture. At times they tried to explain their experience and to discover the way to teach it to others. Their doctrines, and the doctrine of Saint John among these, are valid only as long as our aims are the same. As soon as we decide, as our age has decided, that their goal is not central to our desires, their writings as doctrine are of interest only to those who decide to be their followers.

Even though we may disagree with their beliefs, there are still a few pages in their works that speak to all of us. When we read the poems of Saint John of the Cross, within the context of his mystical experience, they are the representation of his experience for all of us. And we can not fail, within the limits of our capacities, to repeat in our imagination the rapture he created, although we may not want to live his experience beyond this imaginative recreation. As another poet might be the poet of love, as a dramatist might make us live through the terror of crime, Saint John of the Cross offers to our imaginations the vicarious possibility of living the experience of mystical union. No other poet has been as successful, although many have tried. We need not read all who have tried or many of them, since one is superior to the rest, and we only want to reproduce in words a fascinating experience which is often foreign to us.

Obviously this way of approaching the writings of Saint John is erroneous because it distorts the truth of his life. It is, however, adjusted to our truth, and we read him, as we read all literature, for what it means to us. It would be easier also, and perhaps more enjoyable than the laborious study of biography and doctrine, to read the lines of his verse and reread them until we are mesmerized by the poetry of Saint John. Many of us have done it. Many more will repeat this experience in years to come. Yet the full richness of the lines may gain from a less undisciplined approach. After studying the events of his life and his times that explain the thought of Saint John of the Cross, we will read his poems in the light of what he lived as a man. The road, it is true, may not be as pleasant; let us hope the rewards at the end will be worth the effort.

## I  *Spain as a World Power*

Saint John of the Cross lived in an age of contrast and conflict. Although he focused his thought on his inner experience, he could not help but feel the impact of the times in which he lived. Royal absolutism was at war with the traditions of seignorial rights; religious fervor contrasted with Machiavellian politics and moral dissolution; old institutions were crumbling to give way to new conceptions of life and society. Religious controversy was often the center of the crises that beset Europe. Spain was affected by every change, of course, but also, as one of the major powers of the time, her influence was felt in every country and her leadership marked the age. The people of Spain seemed almost obsessed with religion, and yet their rulers sought political power and used every military and diplomatic recourse at their disposal for the achievement of secular aims of aggrandizement.

Long before the birth of Saint John, Ferdinand of Aragon and Isabella of Castile had set the stage for the emergence of Spain as a world power. For centuries the country had been divided into independent kingdoms continually at war with the Moorish invaders and among themselves, until the marriage of Ferdinand and Isabella brought together the largest of these kingdoms. The Catholic Monarchs—a name given to them by

the Pope and used with affection by their subjects—succeeded
in uniting the whole Peninsula, with the exception of Portugal,
in 1492, by taking Granada from the Moors. In the same year,
Columbus claimed the New World in the name of Isabella and
the Crown of Castile. From this would emerge one of the largest
and most powerful empires in history.

Besides carrying their power across the seas, Ferdinand and
Isabella had to establish their authority and regulate the society
inside Spain with "men-at-arms in the field, bishops in their
pontificals, robbers on the gallows."[1] The Catholic Monarchs
succeeded in curbing the power of the nobles, who for centuries
had imposed their will on peasants and kings alike, by taking
away their political monopoly while allowing them to retain
their seignorial privileges, including exemption from taxes and
ownership of the land. Consequently, even though the noblemen
could no longer control the government, they owned ninety-
seven percent of the land while they comprised some two or
three percent of the population.[2] The disparity between the
great wealth of the few and the extreme poverty of most of the
population made the continual struggle for survival of  Saint
John's family the rule rather than the exception. In this society,
the Church was the only force devoted to the task of improving
the lot of the people through charity. The sick and the old
could usually find refuge and help only in the hospitals and
asylums of the Church.

At the same time, the Catholic Monarchs sought to put an
end to rampant banditry on the highways through the revival
of a semi-religious institution of the Middle Ages: the *Santa
Hermandad* (Holy Brotherhood). The *Hermandad* acted as
both police and judge, and, since its usual penalty was either
mutilation or tortured death, it quickly made travel and commerce safe and made royal authority unquestioned throughout
the land.

After putting its own house in order, Spain was to have little
time to enjoy prosperity, though, since its next king, Charles V,
was also the ruler of the Low Countries, parts of Italy, the New
World, and was elected—thanks to a twist of fate and the use
of the Spanish treasury—Emperor of the Holy Roman Empire.
This ancient title gave Charles V little authority over the
numerous princes of Germany, but many real or imaginary

commitments to the defense of the Catholic faith. Charles V had the aspiration to become the universal monarch that European political thought had been dreaming of throughout the Middle Ages. His large empire could never be pacified, however, and most of his life was spent in religious and political wars that drained Spain of men and wealth. His first action as a young king had been the appointment of Flemish noblemen to important public offices in Spain, and his first rebuff was the rebellion of his subjects. Many Spaniards refused to accept a king who favored foreigners and disregarded traditional local rights. Their *comunidades* or cities revolted. Charles V succeeded eventually in putting down this civil war because of the dissension within the ranks of the rebels and the superiority of the government's armies. Although it became increasingly difficult to exact the taxes necessary for his extensive campaigns against Protestants, Moslems, the French, and even the Pope, his subjects never again objected in open rebellion to their contribution in men and gold to the building of the European empire that was so inimical to their own needs and desires.

Unlike Charles V who was a cosmopolitan emperor, his son Philip II was a national king. On the abdication of his father in 1557, Philip retreated to the geographic center of Spain and governed his empire from his desk. Germany had been given to his uncle, but the Low Countries continued to be a source of unrest, and wars against his rebellious subjects there were continuous. But these two men of power and war were also men of religious fervor to the extreme of fanaticism: Charles V retired to a monastery in Yuste to spend the last months of his life in meditation, and Philip II is said to have been a man of intense inner life devoted to the examination and analysis of his faith.

Philip attended personally to every matter of official business from the problems of an individual subject to the planning and execution of his massive campaigns against the Turk or the Crown of England. It is no wonder that his correspondence was so voluminous that special archives had to be built to house it. He had absolute control of the country because he was the only one who knew everything that was going on. During his reign, he had the famous palace of El Escorial built. The vastness and symmetry of this monument give an idea of his ambition, as well as of his cold and mathematical turn of mind. For instance, when he had to choose a capital for his kingdoms, he decided to place the seat of government in the geometric center of the Peninsula, disregarding history, economics, or social reality. The legend of a melancholic and vacillating Philip may be exaggerated, but his fanaticism, austerity, and cruelty molded the Spain that Saint John knew. While these two men never met, they were both products and creators of the environment of extreme religiosity that characterized Spain in the second half of the sixteenth century.

Lest we should be satisfied with a simple view of the past, it must be remembered that Philip II was not only the austere and ascetic king severely dressed in black that legend has emphasized. In spite of his timidity, or because of it, he could indulge in tastes of wealth and luxury. His couriers brought numerous works of art from all the countries of Europe to adorn his palaces. His favorite painter was "El Bosco," the Flemish Hieronymus Bosch, whose "Garden of Delights" the King admired. In this painting Bosch revels in showing the many possibilities of punishment for the monstrous sins of lust. Bodies are engulfed in horrid tortures or encapsulated in the moment of joy and punishment. But we should not be tempted into an easy explanation of the character of the inscrutable king. We must remember also that he loved the triumphant flesh of the nudes of Tiziano, whose mythological paintings he treasured. Only in apparent contradiction, of course, his taste moved from apocalyptic damnation to the seduction of Danae by Jupiter or the abduction of a nymph.

And Philip II was also the defender of the faith. His armies and their cruelty were feared in Europe, Africa, and America. And yet he upheld the Gospel of Love and protected the reformers who were persecuted for their humility and faith. War and piety went hand in hand in the Spain of Philip II, in which Saint John had to live his dream of the complete understanding of beatitude.

## II   The Church in Spain in the Sixteenth Century

In sixteenth-century Spain it was almost universally accepted that obedience to the king was dependent on obedience to God. Political and religious orthodoxy were considered to go hand in hand because "when a subject slips into heresy . . . like an

uncontrolled horse, he will forget his obedience to the king."[3]
Either this theory preceded the practice of religious persecution
or religious persecution was justified in this theory: in either
case the most tolerant European country in the recent Middle
Ages became the center of the bloodiest persecution of minorities
and dissenters.

In 1492 some ten percent or less of Spain's total population
was comprised of minorities: Jews, Moors, and Jews converted
to Catholicism or *conversos*. Religious differences and suspicions
against late *conversos* had always been sources of friction, but
officials in the government and noblemen had protected these
minorities, and, unlike France and England, Spain had not
expelled the Jews from its territory. In spite of an official policy
of tolerance, popular resentment against the Jews was deep.
Riots were not unknown. The populace resented the powerful
positions of some Jews in the Court or in society and singled
out the tax collectors, money lenders, and counselors in Court
as pretexts for their savage attacks. Noblemen and ecclesiastical
authorities could not control the people and finally gave way.
With the territorial unification of Spain, popular zeal and
fanaticism prevailed on the Monarchs, who in 1492 decreed the
expulsion of the Jews, despite the serious economic setback
entailed by the loss of their most important bankers, merchants,
and artisans.

The remaining minority of Moors was also feared. In this
case, people feared something besides the threat of an alien
religion to an established cult. Turkish attacks in the Medi-
terranean and frequent acts of piracy on the coasts of Spain
reminded Spaniards of their vulnerability. The country's Moors
helped in these attacks or at least were believed to be ready
to help, keeping the fear of a second invasion of the Peninsula
very much alive in the minds of the Spaniards. The Catholic
Monarchs thought the conversion of the Moors was sufficient
guarantee of loyalty. But Philip II realized he had to be more
forceful. The *moriscos*—as the Moors converted to Christianity
were called—had proved to be rebellious politically and to hold
to the secret practice of the Moslem religious cult. Despite the
consequences, the Crown tried to enforce edicts banning the
use of the Arabic language and Moorish dress because the King
"valued religion more than revenue."[4] The King's troops were

victorious in the "war of fire and blood" that ensued. The very violence of the rebellion made it necessary in 1609 for the government to resort to the expulsion of the Moors, although Spain stood to lose her best artisans and agricultural experts. Many Moors and Jews chose to stay and become loyal subjects and good observants of the official religion. But they had to face a new scourge at the service of intolerance and fanaticism: the Inquisition.

The Spanish Inquisition had been founded in 1478. While it represented the continuation of a medieval institution founded in France to punish Albigensian heretics, Ferdinand and Isabella gave the Inquisition a new and different form, as they subjected it to direct royal control. Its function was to watch over the purity of the faith, making certain that heretics should not be allowed to contaminate a society that was desperately trying to become completely uniform. Although posterity may have exaggerated the cruelty of the Inquisitors, it is undeniable that in their zeal they resorted to procedures repugnant both because of their stupidity and their cruelty. If the accused heretic did not confess, he was often condemned to be burned at the stake in an *auto-da-fe*, "an elaborate public solemnity, carefully devised to inspire awe for the mysterious authority of the Inquisition, and to impress the population with a wholesome abhorrence of heresy, by representing in so far as it could the tremendous drama of the Day of Judgment."[5] By the mid-sixteenth century the Inquisition became an awesome bureaucratic machine that escaped the control of its creators.

This attempt to purify the country by exacting uniform obedience was paralleled by a process of reform of the Spanish Church. During the sixteenth century, the Spanish Church underwent changes that amounted to revolution. The relaxation of the rules in most monastic orders had been so pervasive that monasteries by the end of the fifteenth century "were often little more than places of diversion."[6] All through the sixteenth century the Reformation in the North was attempting to bring a new understanding of Christianity and instigate new practices. Spain tried a reform that called for a return to what was remembered or perhaps only imagined as a golden era of the same Church, without challenging the dogma in any way. But a return to an older and stricter observance was not always welcome. On one hand, many monks refused to give up their lives of pleasure. Many a spiritual director, on the other hand, sincerely believed that an excessively rigorous discipline could be dangerous and lead to insanity rather than sanctity. Suicide and mental derangement were known to exist in the strictest Orders; and possession by the devil—a common occurrence in this period—could and was interpreted as a form of mental imbalance. Not everyone who opposed this reform then was debauched. Many priests believed that a more relaxed rule was better for the development of sincerity in the practices of religious life.

But the Spanish Church chose the path of reform. In recognition of Ferdinand and Isabella's words and deeds in the name of Christendom, the Pope heeded their pleas, and for the first time in Western Europe the Spanish monarchs were given power over all ecclesiastical appointments. Ferdinand and Isabella were conscientious and made many appointments on the basis of merit, rather than because of wealth or personal influence.

Isabella found able assistance for her work of reform in the man she named to be her confessor and the highest prelate of Spain, Cardinal Ximenes de Cisneros. This man, single-mindedly and without support from other clerics, dedicated himself to religious reform. Because of his interest in mysticism, he gathered around him a small group of Franciscan friars and sought mystic experience with them by observing the stricter primitive practices of the Order. He wore poor friar's robes and ate frugal meals until the Pope ordered him to "maintain the dignity of his rank in his external life."[7] Under him it became law that "priests had to live in the monastery and confess as often as possible to be purer to celebrate Mass. Every Sunday clerics were under penalty of a fine to preach the Gospel to the faithful and to instruct the children."[8] The program for reform encountered formidable opposition even from the more conscientious Franciscans, but their attacks only made Isabella support Cisneros all the more.

Besides attempting to return to the older stricter practices of the Orders, Cisneros also wanted the Church to benefit from the new emphasis on theological education and biblical study. To raise the level of the Spanish episcopate, Cisneros established the University of Alcalá. As in the other institutions of higher learning of the time in Bologna, Paris, Oxford, and Salamanca, the main focus in this University was theological studies. At first, the University encouraged diverse approaches, and Cisneros even offered a professorship to Erasmus. By the time Saint John of the Cross went there as Rector in 1570, however, intellectual freedom in Spain had been curbed.

At the same time that the Spanish Church was trying to solve its own problems and arguing the benefits of reform, and the Nordic Church was being divided by the efforts of Lutherans and other Protestants, there arose in Spain a new form of religious experience. The Catholic hierarchy opposed these people who believed in a personal satisfaction in their religious desires. Unfortunately, since this was an age of name calling, their heresy was immediately labelled "Lutheranism," although it had little if any relation to the thinking of Luther. The *illuminati* (Illuminists), people who can see an inner light, as history has come to call them, were not followers of any foreign leader. They were rather a motley group, without a well-defined set of beliefs, that grew up in response to the needs of the human soul which were made much more acute at that time by the religious hysteria kindled by reform and persecution. The climate was one of obsession with religious values, and, as a result, all kinds of approaches to the need for salvation were to be expected.

In the turbulent religious crisis of the sixteenth century, the simplicity of a former age which viewed the conflict of two religions—the Christian and the Mohammedan—as central was no longer tenable. We must remember that even before 1492 this view had been an over-simplification. The irruption of the varied pagan ways of the recently discovered world and the new attention to Classical pagan letters brought on a sense of danger and a need for reaffirmation. In one way or another, most heretics of the century tried to redefine the meaning of salvation by reaffirming the possibility of a personal salvation, outside the ritual. They were attempting to assuage the doubts and the fears of those who could not comprehend a life without the bondage of thought to belief.

The *illuminati* believed in their salvation through their own efforts. They did not feel the need of a mediator in their relationship to God and sought their own form of direct inner communication with Him by means of—as one member described it—"being completely empty of ourselves so that God could fill our hearts."[9] Such unorthodox inwardness and disregard for religious ceremony filled the Inquisition with horror. In 1525 the Inquisition brought the leading Illuminists to trial and in the same year banned the writings of Luther from Spain.

While the works of Luther could not pass the Pyrenees, the writing of the Catholic humanist Erasmus of Rotterdam quickly took root in Spain. Erasmism was the intellectuals' answer to the same need for an inner faith that the Illuminists had expressed. But some zealous Spanish theologians could see heresy in Erasmism and placed it in the same category as Lutheranism and Illuminism. Although the meeting of theologians they convoked in Valladolid in 1527 failed to condemn Erasmism, as they had desired, it marked the beginning of the end. Suspicion, fear, and disillusionment mounted, and in 1535 the Inquisition took further steps towards imposing orthodoxy on the country, and the leading Erasmists were tried and condemned.

During the first half of the sixteenth century, belief in eventual religious reconciliation had kept hope and openness alive. With this goal in mind, the Spaniards played a leading role in the Council of Trent convoked in 1545. Before the Council's deliberations ended almost twenty years later, the Catholic world had had to accept the impossibility of their dream of Christian unity and recognize the establishment of the Protestant Church. The Council forged the arms with which the Catholic world prepared to fight the irreconcilable Protestants: the *Index*, the Jesuit Order, and the Inquisition. Throughout Europe a new militantism and dogmatism defined and hardened both camps. Philip II was haunted by the necessity of assuring Spain's ideological impermeability, and his fears were exacerbated by the pressure of the French Huguenots and the insurrections of his own subjects in the Netherlands to the north and by the revolts of *moriscos* and the ominous threat of Arab invasion to the south. These fears put Philip and the Spanish Inquisition on twenty-four hour guard over the souls of their subjects. The Spanish *Index* of 1559 was notably more severe than its predecessors, and, among other works, it banned Erasmus' most famous, the *Enchiridion*. Censorship and prohibition of foreign study helped to isolate Spain from major European intellectual currents. The militant new Order of the Chuch, the Company

of Jesus, was founded by a Spaniard, Saint Ignatius of Loyola.
It found fertile ground in Spain where it soon acquired ascend-
ancy over the political powers, and where it exerted enormous
influence until its expulsion almost two centuries later. The
Inquisition operated more and more as an autonomous and all-
powerful machine, arresting and  punishing many who twenty-
five years before had been counselors to the King and imposing
even stricter control over the *moriscos*.

The intensity of their own religious experience made many
Spaniards seek further reforms in the Orders. Saint Theresa,
anxious to restore the austerities of primitive rule, founded the
first house of the Discalced Carmelites in Avila in 1562; by her
death in 1582 she had founded fourteen priories and sixteen
convents. There was great impetus too for the establishment of
charitable foundations, and by 1590 there were six hundred
charitable hospitals similar to the one founded by Saint John
of God in Granada in 1537. Such religious intensity and social
concern not only sprang from the Tridentine doctrines, but also
from the deep-rooted and traditional Spanish religious fervor
that had sought expression through Illuminism and Erasmism.
For many members of the religious Orders, the most natural
expression of the vital inner experience of their faith was mysticism. In 1559, many of the works of the mystics were placed on
the *Index*, because such experiences were feared as a prelude
to heresy. But later the Inquisition reversed this decision when
it saw that mysticism appeared to be the natural tendency of
the age and that nuns and priests could hardly be considered
the allies of foreign heretics.

III    *The Literature of Spain in the Sixteenth Century*

At the same time that Spain was becoming an empire, a new
vitality was felt in all the enterprises of the Peninsula, from
commerce to religious thinking. All fields of learning and all
forms of art and thought flourished in this period of strenuous
activity. Artists from other countries, mainly Italy and Flanders,
teachers and scholars as well as men of thought and of action,
came to the cities of Spain attracted by their new wealth and
their lively interest in creating and building. The language of
the Peninsula, up to now splintered in many dialects, strove to
acquire a new cohesiveness in order to serve the need of this

increased activity. Before this time, writers had preferred Latin for learned treatises and Portuguese for the writing of lyric poetry because the dialects of Castile seemed to lack the flexibility and refinement they desired. But now they undertook the task of turning Castilian into the dominant dialect in the Peninsula.

The rules of linguistic usage were codified at the end of the fifteenth century. Antonio de Nebrija or Lebrija, a professor at the oldest university of Spain in Salamanca, was the first grammarian of the Castilian language. His work was published in 1492 and was the first attempt to study a modern language systematically. Until then, grammatical studies had been restricted to the discussion of Latin, Greek, or Hebrew, but Nebrija saw the need for a new task. His intention was to set forth the rules of grammar for the Spanish language so that it could be taught to the peoples to be converted and ruled by the Catholic Monarchs. In his prologue and dedication to Queen Isabella, Nebrija makes clear that his book is intended as a tool of empire to be used by foreigners who would need to learn a language not their own.

The idea of empire is part of the life of Spain at this moment. Centralized government and common enterprises had been a dream in the Middle Ages; their reality marks the beginning of a new period: the Renaissance. The cultural revolution of this moment in Europe, and particularly in Spain, is a complex phenomenon, more difficult to define than the simple explanation of its name seems to imply. There is indeed in the Renaissance a rebirth of interest in the writings of the Classics of Greece and Rome, not entirely forgotten in the Middle Ages; there is also a turning away from theological and theoretical study to observation and scientific undertakings. Yet the new preoccupations do not exclude the old beliefs, and the spirit of the times can best be described through the effects produced by the conflicts of the old and the new. The Humanists, scholars who devoted their efforts to the study and interpretation of Greek and Latin literatures, were interested in the secular or humane letters, but they also helped in the establishing of religious texts. They were often the leaders in the developing universities of Spain, Italy, and France, where the study of religion was a central requirement of the curriculum. At the same time, the prelates of the Church continued their exegesis of biblical texts and added to their learning all they could assimilate from this new Humanism. It was not unlikely that an ecclesiastic should translate love poems from the Latin at the same time as he composed books on devotional subjects. And there was no contradiction in his mind.

There were rapid and profound changes in the literature of Spain at the end of the fifteenth and beginning of the sixteenth century. There was a new vastness and complexity in thought and a new richness in language. Activity in all genres was so intense thereafter and the excellence of works produced was such that the period has come to be called the Golden Age of Spanish literature. It is difficult to establish the limits of a period, especially when it is characterized mostly by the superiority of its products. But doubtless the first great book of the Golden Age was the *Tragicomedia de Calisto y Melibea,* published in 1499 and reworked in several editions during the first years of the sixteenth century.

Calisto and Melibea, like Romeo and Juliet in the English tradition, are two young lovers doomed to destruction in an uncomprehending world. Their love is earthly and is punished within the morality of the Middle Ages. In this long novel in dialogue form, or long drama as it can be considered, the lovers are brought together by the evil force of a go-between called Celestina, a character so powerful and all-pervading that the book has popularly been known by her name rather than by the original title. Her sorcery and evil belong to a past that will not be forgotten in Europe for many a century, but the sighs of love of Calisto are echoes of a new conception popularized by the poetry of Petrarch. Melibea's final suicide and her recollection of ancient philosophers, about whom she talks in one of the great soliloquies of the book, belong also to the novelties of the Renaissance. The choice of pleasure over the dictates of duty in these characters is a clear sign of a change in cultural patterns, in spite of the author's adherence to the morality of punishment. Fernando de Rojas, the probable author of this book, combines in his artistry themes and attitudes of the past and the present. His language is also the combination of a new latinized rhetoric and the racy proverbial language of the common people. With the *Tragicomedia de Calisto y Melibea* Spanish prose comes of age, and, because of its dialogue form, the beginnings of a theatre can also be traced to its success. The following 150 years see the flowering of all literary genres in the Spanish language.

The opposite views of life that the idealized lovers and the underworld of the go-between represent will be present thereafter in all Spanish literature. Sometimes the same author or book will be torn between these extremes, sometimes an author will choose to follow one or the other of these roads to its ultimate meaning and to its formal perfection. The picaresque novel of the sixteenth century is perhaps the best example of an interest in the life of the lowborn, their predicaments, their adventures, and their struggle to acquire the peace of mind that will permit them to live in an unfriendly society. The poetry of this century, on the contrary, will take up the Petrarchan views of love and idealize woman in an atmosphere of artifice.

It is in this century also that the writers of Spain turn with greatest fervor to the analysis of religious life. In them, obviously, the idealization of subjects and the artifices of language seem to be necessary. Yet, the writers of religious treatises came from the people and often used the raciest of languages. As a result, in many of their works, especially in the prose of Saint Theresa of Jesus, we can find the concerns and expression of everyday life as well as the exaltations of rapture and rhetoric. In the same way, the poetry of Saint John of the Cross that we will study seems to carry the ideal to regions far removed from the incidents and unpleasantness of everyday life. And yet his language often has the richness of a tradition alive with observation and attention to the world of objects and things human. His sensuous imagery and bejewelled language are in conflict with the extreme purity of his thought only on the surface. There is a deeper unity that binds his doctrine and its expression, which we will try to understand in the following chapters.

CHAPTER 2

# Apprenticeship and Contemplation

*Entréme donde no supe,*
*Y quedéme no sabiendo,*
*Toda sciencia trascendiendo.*
> Coplas hechas sobre un éxtasis
> de alta contemplación.

(I entered I knew not where
And I remained, knowing nothing, where
All science was transcended.
> Verses written upon an Ecstasy
> of High Contemplation.)

WHEN, in the twenty-sixth year of his life, Juan de Yepes embraced the strictest rules of religious life, he could anticipate nothing but suffering until his death. Although he was young, and perhaps impetuous in his decision, there never was any hesitation or regret in the years to follow. If anything, he deplored afterwards only the interruptions and the demands on his time that drew him away from solitude, mortification, and prayer. His decision stemmed from mature reflection and gave direction to his whole life and shape to his work.

There must have been a long period of preparation for this decision. Certainly the experiences of his childhood and adolescence had to be such as to prompt in Juan de Yepes a desire to renounce whatever the world might have had to offer, whatever lures of pleasure and wealth his fantasy could conjure. Early in life he was already resigned to forfeit the minimum birthright of strife and hope that is the lot of even the poorest of men. It is not known, for he never told others about it, whether or not there was a long struggle in his soul before he reached his decision. Perhaps the desire for peace silenced in the young Juan de Yepes all other ambitions from early in his chilhood.

27

Since we know little, almost nothing, about the inner life of Saint John before he decided to set down in writing the emotions and reflections of his maturity, we have no way of pursuing a process of evolution that might explain the flowering of thought and poetry of his thirties and forties. All we can do is to trace signs in the few events recorded and try to interpret them. The external events of his childhood and youth may serve as indications, but are not accompanied by recollections in diary or letters. That he felt no need to rationalize and explain to contemporaries or posterity may be in itself the best proof of his sincerity and humility. Indeed, Juan de Yepes had decided to retire into an absolute silence, into a life that would leave no trace. He desired nothing but to be forgotten by men.

A few months before his decision to become a contemplative monk, Juan de Yepes had been ordained a priest of the Catholic Church. He could have chosen to continue in the service of his calling as an active member of the most powerful institution in his country—at this moment in the history of Spain, almost one-fourth of the population was in one way or another attached to the Church[1]—but he felt the need of something different. This need, though, must not be understood as a mere renunciation or as a way of imposing silence on the activity of his powerful mind. He was affirming a way of life in which he believed and through which he thought salvation was to be found.

Juan de Yepes had made up his mind to go further in the exploration of religious life. After being ordained, he desired to enter a life of utmost solitude and silence and considered becoming a Carthusian. We owe this information about Saint John's intentions to the diligence of Saint Theresa who was an indefatigable writer and chronicler of events.[2] On her advice, Juan de Yepes decided to remain in the Order of Carmel, to which he belonged, and to embark on its Reform. His choice was to prove somewhat disillusioning, as he had to enter many a tempestuous battle before he could find the peace he hoped for, but he never wavered in his vows. His writings, then, must be understood in the light of a decision he reached before his thirtieth year and which was from then on the guiding principle of his life.

The turmoils and dissension in his Order, the struggle for power, and the persecutions he was to suffer never touched the inner peace of John of the Cross. His life was devoted to contemplative thought, to meditation and prayer, and even the activity of writing was something he did not need, and was undertaken mainly out of regard for others. Poetry was apparently of little interest to him in his youth, and it is only as an apparent interlude in his later activities that Saint John wrote a few poems, which are considered the best in the Spanish language. He had never aimed at literary success, and indeed his works were not even published during his life. He had no intentions either of writing on philosophical or theological themes; he only ventured into fashioning commentaries on his own poetry in order to help the novices in their understanding of the religious life they had undertaken. Almost against his will, these commentaries became treatises of doctrinal exposition of theology.

As we have indicated, Saint John wrote poetry to express the most intimate experiences of his solitude and treatises to explain this poetry. Neither poetry nor treatises were a source of pride or a form of achievement to him. They were only a record of his life of contemplation in which the inner pursuit of knowledge had taken him to an awareness of the power of the mind seldom experienced in such fullness. His experience was one of mystic knowledge because it transcended the normal paths of logical understanding. Therefore, the strange relationship of contemplation and mystic experience to the refinements of poetic expression should be studied only as affecting the form of his writings, never as a part of his life, since Saint John of the Cross deliberately shunned any involvement in literary ambitions. His biographers then have to study a process influenced by many forces and leading ultimately to knowledge through ecstasy and only taking at one point the forms and conventions of literature to fill them with the outpouring of his emotions.

Saint John never had anything to do with the usual literary circles. He was devoted entirely to the perfection of his inner life, or incidentally, to the affairs of his Order. The external events, the travelling, the struggle for the independence of his group against the old Carmelites, the teaching of novices, all the duties of his station, were for him only accidental; necessary, but not essential to his undertaking. His vocation as a religious was to perfect his soul to the point of annihilation of whatever

kept him from a complete union with God. This pursuit of
perfection and complete understanding of the divine is a
discipline and an aim that has been known to all religions. His
mysticism is, therefore, in no way different from the attainment
and the experiences of other mystics, except that it has become
known to us in special ways both through his doctrinal treatises
and his poetry. But it could have remained unsaid, and, as far
as Saint John himself cared, the loss of his writings would have
made absolutely no difference in his determination to strive for
perfection.

The life of a mystic must exist in itself and for itself before
any expression or sign of such an inner adventure can reach
others. Often it is only under extreme pressure, under orders from
superiors even, that the person who has achieved ecstasy decides
he must communicate his experience. The writings of Saint
John are even more reticent than those of other mystics. He had
no desire to explain himself or his position in them. "Where
Saint Theresa is prepared in the cause of charity to expose her
intimate spiritual life that others may gain from her experience,
Saint John of the Cross from motives of humility allows no trace
of his own personal history to obtrude, at least in identifiable
form."[3]

Our task of exploring in his life the origin and formation of
his thought becomes then immensely difficult. After surveying
the external events of his life, we can only imagine the moment
in which he reached that secret abode where in ignorance he
was *toda sciencia trascendiendo,* transcending all knowledge.
Did he bring this inner knowledge to the studies and reflection
of a monk's life, or did he find this super-science after a long and
painful search? We may never know for certain, and this is,
perhaps, the central mystery he wanted to bequeath to future
students. Whether we start from knowledge or arrive at
knowledge does not really matter: it is only important to know
that we want to know. The problem posed to the biographer
is to ascertain how his desire led the young Juan de Yepes
through the tumult of life, how it gave him the inner peace
of his writings. In this sense, every reader of Saint John of the
Cross will have to think out for himself a spiritual biography
that will fit into the few facts of his life as we know them.

## I  *A Child of Poverty*

The vocation of Saint John of the Cross was that of contemplation. Although he had to take an active part in the affairs of his Order, he did  so only against his wishes. For this reason, at least on the surface, his thought and his writings seem little related to the events of his own life or to the tumult of his surroundings. Nevertheless, the method of his approach to spiritual life and the form of his expression can be understood only through the study of a life subjected to the accidents and designs of the society in which it was lived. Even though he seems to us completely removed from passion, his writings are a product of his times, and, as in the case of every man, the experiences life forced on him shaped and gave meaning to the achievements he strove for and the goals he attained.

From the very beginning of Juan de Yepes' religious life, and increasingly with the passage of years, the young man gave evidence of the strongest will. In his maturity his immovable will gave an impression of terror in its fixedness; it was awe-inspiring with something supernatural in its strength. And at the same time there was tenderness and a childlike sweetness in his character. Neither the strength nor the innocence of his character can be explained except within the circumstances that surrounded the child and the youth before he made the extraordinary decisions that were to guide his life and his actions.

Juan de Yepes was born in 1542 in the small town of Fontiveros in the province of Avila in Old Castile, at approximately the same distance to the north of the capital city of Avila and to the east of Salamanca. But the thirty to forty miles that separated the town from the religious center of Avila or the University of Salamanca were, in the sixteenth century, much more formidable than they seem today. People could, however, walk or ride from one to the other of these towns with relative ease, and, as we will often see, the activities of the priests of the Order of Carmel took them from one to another of the many towns and cities of central Spain.

Fontiveros was and still is a very small and quiet country town lost in the somber and arid landscape of Old Castile. The austerity and dryness of the plateau are somewhat relieved in the vicinity of Fontiveros—which is a relatively fertile region—but the surroundings are still the famous brown and hard outlines that nurtured the asceticism of the monks and the endurance of the soldiers of Castile.

In this town first, and in neighboring cities later, the central experience of Saint John's childhood was the experience of poverty. His poverty must have been very special and extreme. He must have known successively different forms of poverty: the poverty of the low-stationed family and its meager ration; the destitution of a fatherless child; the shocking contrast of a charity hospital in a city of luxury and trade; the vows of mendicant poverty of an Order; in short, all the possibilities and varieties of poverty.

Not much is known about Saint John's family. His father, Gonzalo de Yepes, belonged to the minor nobility of the town of Yepes near Toledo, in New Castile, and hence was entitled to property and wealth. But he was disowned by his family because he decided to marry a peasant girl, Catalina Alvarez. They settled in her home town of Fontiveros. Since members of the gentry usually learned no trade, Gonzalo had to apply himself to a trade new to him. He became a weaver, perhaps because his wife's family were weavers, and managed to make a scant living. Three boys were born to the couple, Francisco, Luis, and Juan, who was the last. In the years of their early childhood, Juan and his brothers must have known the frugality verging on destitution of a worker's family in a small town of that age and place. There must have been also the love and quiet happiness of a family in reduced circumstances trying to help one another. Francisco must have begun to work as a weaver early in childhood, and Luis and Juan were probably looking forward to the day they would be of some help.

When Juan was not quite six years of age, Gonzalo de Yepes died, and Catalina had to take care of her three boys the best she could. How the young mother could manage without property, income, or friends, is difficult to imagine. For five years after the death of her husband she travelled in the vicinity without finding a way to support her children. She attempted to settle in Arévalo, some seventeen miles to the northeast of Fontiveros, but the death of Luis and her dire need drove her on. It is said that at one point, in the town of Gálvez, near Toledo, where she had gone hoping that her husband's relatives might help her, she left Francisco with distant relatives who promised to take care of him, but had to take him with her again when she realized that he was being mistreated. After years of wandering and suffering, Catalina settled in Medina del Campo in the neighboring province of Valladolid, some twenty-odd miles to the north of Arévalo. She made her living as a weaver, and Francisco, who was old enough to help, became a weaver also.

Juan was, at this point, some eleven or twelve years of age, an obedient and alert boy who, according to the customs of the time and to the station of his family, was supposed to prepare himself to earn a livelihood. He was apprenticed to a wood-carver, then to a painter, then to a carpenter. Juan seemed to enjoy working in these trades and even showed some promise. He was skilled and tried to outdo himself in works of artistic merit as well as good craftsmanship. And yet he was not happy in any of these crafts and had no inclination to join his family in the profession of weaving.

It does seem odd that Juan should not have succeeded in any craft or helped his family in their poverty. Some biographers postulate a great love of learning in the twelve-year-old boy, but no document confirms this. Since he had not yet gone to school, this vocation could not really have existed. The ascertained facts are different: only after being apprenticed to several craftsmen did the boy go to school. Was he a problem child for his mother? Did she wonder what his unwillingness to stick to a trade would bring to him in the future?

Catalina and her two boys had settled in Medina del Campo some time between 1552 and 1554. Apparently they found some relief from their financial distress, since both she and Francisco were able to work as weavers. Yet among the inhabitants of Medina, "skilled, prosperous, and contented,"[4] the newcomers must have suffered great poverty. When Juan was twelve, nevertheless, his mother managed to give him the necessary leisure to attend the free Jesuit school for the children of the poor. He impressed his teachers with his obedience, humility, and ability to learn.

A few months of respite between his attempts to learn a trade and his finding a livelihood were spent in this school. He probably learned here reading, writing, and Latin grammar. That a boy of twelve or thirteen should show an inclination for arid studies of this type is in itself extraordinary; even more so if we reflect that Juan de Yepes had no example at home since his brother Francisco did not show any interest in any kind of learning; this was true even after the death of Saint John, when he had already witnessed the extraordinary accomplishments of his brother. Francisco de Yepes was a simple soul, very devout and extremely devoted to his family, but scarcely aware of books or learning. He seemed though to have had a good ear and to have known many songs. Perhaps the reminiscences of popular melodies in the poetry of Saint John owe something to the singing and reciting by his relatives at home when as a child he spent evenings watching his mother and brother at their weaving.

The shock of comparing his very humble household and the pomp of the town has not been recorded for us by Juan de Yepes. As a matter of fact, he seems to have been unaware of the existence of luxury in the world. Yet in a family of indigent weavers, a young boy who has grown up without the support of a father could not fail to realize the difference between his own destitution and the wealth of Medina del Campo. The city had been for a long time a center of commerce. There were within the walled town four palaces and more than two hundred mansions, and the suburbs contained a larger population than that of the inner city of 1,240 streets to which fourteen gates gave access. In the middle of the sixteenth century the city of Medina del Campo was one of the most prosperous in Spain and, perhaps, in the whole of Western Europe. It had a population of over 15,000 and boasted of the largest *Plaza Mayor* in Spain. Its printing presses were the most active in the country. The city was the trading center for the region. Twice a year, in May and October, large international fairs that lasted nearly four weeks, were held there.

To these ancient fairs of Medina came merchants from all over Spain, from major cities and small towns, wholesalers and retailers, cattle dealers and shipping magnates. The smallest trading posts sent their representatives to Medina. Merchants from the region and from afar came to trade their silks and their wools, the fine Cordovan leathers as well as the silks from Valencia. From France came fine Cambric linens and jewels; all kinds of cloth, especially linens, came from the Low Countries;

Flemish tapestries and pearls from the Orient were displayed and traded. Parchment, velvets, silver, foodstuffs of all kinds, Chinese delicacies brought from mysterious Cathay by the Portuguese, iron, pottery, wood carvings, and all imaginable products of man's industry and skill were traded in the colorful streets of Medina, which were carefully assigned by law to each trade, skill, or product.[5]

Here began also a system of symbolic payments, drafts, and I.O.U.'s—deferred from fair to fair—that was soon imitated by many trading fairs in Spain and abroad and became the model for banking operations of the times.[6] In these fairs all luxury and human vanity were congregated. The misery that usually accompanies artificial prosperity was also to be seen here. Hosts of vagabonds and beggars plagued the town, and thieves and marauders were numerous and arrogant. The shining wealth of the commercial town had its counter in crime, poverty, and disease.

The young Juan de Yepes must have been dazzled by the sumptuousness of the houses of Medina del Campo and by the lavish display of jewels and fine clothes. Yet his reaction, even as a child, does not seem to have been one of desire for wealth or envy of the power and well-being surrounding him. There was no greed or malice in his soul, but, as it were, only a sadness that separated him from even the vicarious enjoyment of luxury.

At the age of twelve, Juan de Yepes must have gone hungry many a time. He found solace, though, in the satisfaction of turning inward and in the solitude of his reading: but it was not the reading of fanciful adventures that captured his imagination. He was seduced by the simple words of the catechism and repeated with joy the monotonous lessons of his school. No wonder his teachers were astonished at his piety and intelligence. They recommended the poor boy to the attention of Antonio Alvarez de Toledo, a wealthy merchant who had donated a fund for a hospital, and brought him in this way a step closer to the fulfillment of his fate.

## II  *"The Hospital de las Bubas"*

The *Hospital de las Bubas* was Antonio Alvarez de Toledo's favorite charity. Those afflicted with hideous pustules or buboes came here to be protected rather than to be nursed or cured. It is quite possible that many of the sick were syphilitic but, given the haphazard diagnosis of the time, leprosy, bubonic plague, tuberculosis, and erysipelas must have been just as common. All those whose sores or ravings made them unwelcome in their homes or in other hospitals came to add their wailing to the hopelessness of the dying or to die in their turn. Medicine held no hope for them; there were no effective drugs, salves, or therapy. Those who had lost a limb could watch another limb rot. Those who had not lost any as yet could see their future in the maimed bodies all around them. And when the pain and the misery were too deep for moaning, they could imitate the silent few who could be manipulated at will into any position, who remained indefinitely in the position the doctors devised for them. This state of catalepsy is little understood today. No wonder it seemed incredible then.

In the *Hospital de las Bubas* of Medina del Campo, many people hid their sicknesses from the world. Epileptic seizures, preceded by inhuman screams, would often amaze the night. In the middle of the day, patients would have a spurt of incredible excitement and, just as suddenly, cease almost all voluntary action. After their volubility, their posturing and gesturing, the mutism of their statuesque position and their extreme compliance with any suggestion, especially if accompanied by a gentle pressure, might have seemed almost a miraculous cure. But then the lethargy and the stupor, the delusions and the hallucinations, the new frenzies and the new lethargies would belie the impression. The young Juan must have watched these human statues with wonder and fear. When a crisis came, when they stopped in any position, standing or sitting, and, looking with vacant eyes, would not stir or speak, did the boy ask himself what fantasies were in their minds? Did the man, years later, wonder what those figures meant? Did his warning against all deceitful forms of belief, against the mistaking of a diseased imagination for the voice of the divinity stem from his acquaintance with auditory and visual hallucinations, with schizophrenia and catalepsy? Certainly, nobody would have guessed then that, centuries later, we would pause in our work to puzzle over the possible influence of what was then a commonplace occurrence on the imaginations of a boy of fourteen.

But we are fortunate in that we know something about the conditions of medicine at that time in the very city where Saint John was working. A famous physician was practicing there. And, although Juan may never have seen or heard Gómez Pereira make the rounds of the wards or discuss the nature of the diseases, we can see through the eyes of a doctor's description the sights the boy could see. This doctor was one of a new kind. He did not go by the book and did not classify according to authority. He tried instead to describe what he saw. Although he was not able to cure—the only remedy for pustules or buboes was a sharp knife—he knew that an accurate description, an objective study could bring the beginning of understanding. And yet, his was not an age of scientific optimism. Research was not expected to bring cure. Medicine was only a way of alleviating pain. Death was not unnecessary and remote as we see it today, but necessary and immediate.

The observations of the physician were accurate. He described how some patients were seized by a strange attack which kept them indefinitely in the position in which they were caught: standing or sitting, their eyes closed or open, and fixedly looking without seeing.[7] The years of 1556 and 1557, moreover, before Saint John had begun his duties at the hospital, were especially bad. A strange epidemic of fevers, characterized by delirium on one hand and apathy on the other, made the mournful corridors of the hospital a study in contrasts. Lethargy or stupor mingled with the frenzy of hallucinations. Again and again, the immutability of one patient and the restlessness of the next one must have wounded the serenity of Juan's sensibility and awakened him to the painful task of observation.

It is in this atmosphere that the sensitive young student saw the reverse side of the luxuries of Medina del Campo. The seignorial mansions, the merchandise and traffic, the silks and the jewels of the marketplace were in sharp contrast with the melancholy and the fevers of the hospital. Yet the young boy did not flee from the sight of the hideous. At least, he did not decide to leave and take up any of the other trades in which he had shown some skill. Did he escape inwardly into the peace of a search for the reasons for such suffering, for the explanation of the cause of misery, or into the surrender to a belief in a justification and an aim for all he saw?

Without his words to tell us, we can only conjecture. Our conjecture in this case, though, may be a better document than diary or memoirs. We can be this boy, we can watch the pus and blood spurt from elephantine legs, and the cataleptic and hieratic figure look past them. We can sense the strength necessary to watch the horrors and turn to the books for an answer. If we linger in the evocation of many hours of hospital toil, we can understand perhaps what faith meant to him, how he could then bear each hideous moment in the belief that it was a necessary part of a beautiful wholenesss, unexplained and unexplainable. His understanding of the divinity as a form of supreme beauty came to him later, as a result of studying the Platonic tradition in writers of his time. But only if we contrast his sufferings and his knowledge of suffering and his search for the ideal beauty can we understand the intensity of his belief. His was never an intellectual definition of the deity, but rather an affirmation of its essence and its beauty crying out from his painful need for it in the loneliness and the pain of a hospital for the demented. When within the walls of a prison cell, some twenty years later, Saint John uttered the most melodious words in his language, he must have answered the need of his youth to illuminate the cruelty of this suffering with the certainty of a world of light and harmony.

Through the years of early adolescence, when other boys play and fight, Juan de Yepes was so humble and quiet and he helped the sick with such uncomplaining devotion that his superiors in the Hospital felt he had to be rewarded. No special vacation or luxury was to be his prize. The spirit of the age as well as the personality of the young boy are revealed to us in the choice of a reward: Juan de Yepes was allowed to spend a couple of hours each day in the Jesuit school of the town listening to Latin lessons. The intensity of his soul and the heroism of his will are manifest in his adding to his daily chores and his daily lessons many hours of candlelight meditation and reading stolen from his sleep.

If we did not know of his laborious day through the narrative of his brother Francisco, we might have believed that Juan had been abandoned by or had abandoned his family. On the contrary, his home life seemed to have been happy and peaceful. His mother, as far as we know, did not complain because her son had chosen a road of sacrifice and humility and not one of ambition and enterprise. Neither his mother nor his brother fully understood the aims of Saint John's mind, but both of them admired his devotion and patience.

Six years in the service of the sick and the poor tempered the young man's soul. Juan continued to study by candlelight, and when he had grown to manhood, he was thought to be capable of the direction of souls. After having been ordained, his benefactor, Alvarez de Toledo, decided to offer him the position of chaplain in the Hospital. Had he accepted, he might have eased the burden of poverty for himself and his family, and, besides, continued with the noble task of helping others. Juan had, however, different plans. He was studying to qualify himself to enter the University of Salamanca. Again, this preparation should not be construed, as would seem logical to us today, as an effort to better his lot in any material way. On the contrary, this dogged will to learn stemmed from a desire of renunciation. He was learning philosophy, rhetoric, Latin, and theology, to prepare himself for an inquiry that leads only to understanding, not to a profession or a career. Something profound and powerful guided him. His inflexible will had decided on his goal, and his next step was to be the beginning of a long search that would bring reward only after the most excruciating physical, psychological, and moral suffering.

## III  *The University of Salamanca*

His years in the *Hospital de las Bubas* had taught Juan de Yepes to curb natural repugnance in dealing with the sick in mind and body. At the same time, he had been able to learn .the rudiments of Latin, rhetoric, and theology in the Jesuit school in town. Besides this learning and his experience with people, he had acquired character. He had worked without rest or hope throughout his childhood and adolescence, and, in 1563, at the age of twenty-one, he was ready to become a priest. To this calling he brought his tenacity, his quiet and unconquerable will, and his desire to help others and to lead souls.

Juan chose to join the Order of Carmel, without any knowledge of the revolutionary views of some of its members who advocated a return to the primitive rules. The Order of Carmel is one of the oldest in the Catholic Church. Its origins go back to the thirteenth century. In its earliest form it was a strict order of eremitical priests, but, by the time Juan de Yepes joined it with the name of Juan de Santo Matía, it had relaxed its rules considerably, although some ten years before there had begun a movement that tried to return to the rigid observances of the past. Teresa de Jesús was the leading force in this movement. At the age of eighteen, Theresa had applied for admission at the Carmelite Convent of the Incarnation in Avila. She lived for some twenty years in the disappointing atmosphere of a convent with slack discipline, but, in 1554, after the death of her father, she turned inward in search of a new discipline.

From 1554 to 1562, Saint Theresa lived in a state of doubt and perplexity. She suffered from a mysterious illness and often fell into trances, which some of her sisters in the convent believed to be caused by the devil. At one time she fell into the state of catalepsy, from which she recovered through what seemed to some a miraculous resurrection. Her trances and her visions continued. In spite of strong opposition, Saint Theresa was able to found, on August 24, 1562, the first Convent of Reformed or Discalced Carmelites. The rules of this branch of the Carmelites were to be much stricter, and included the wearing of coarse sandals to distinguish them from the sisters of the old observance.

In 1563, the young friar who joined the Order of Carmel in Medina del Campo was unaware of the foundation of this branch in Avila. For Juan de Yepes, when he joined the Order, had probably only vague notions about its past and little knowledge about its workings in the present. He probably believed, as legend had it then, that the Order had been founded by Elias on Mount Carmel; that members of his Order were present at Saint Peter's first sermon on Pentecost, were converted, and built a chapel on Mount Carmel in honor of the Virgin, who enrolled herself in the Order. Perhaps the devotion to Mary, a signal trait of the Carmelites, prompted the youth to join this order before leaving for Salamanca to pursue university studies.

Of this period of his life, before leaving for Salamanca, we know only the external details. No record has been left of his attitude towards the town in which his services, according to his brother's recollection, were so highly prized. But precisely because the friar never remembers his services, his sufferings, or even his joy in his work, we must conjecture that these years hide the mystery of the cause for his decision. And his daily contact with the hideous, his humble acceptance of God's will in every disease and in every death, needs to be recalled slowly, almost with lingering and morbid curiosity, to understand how his will was steeled against temptations. The decision to join a monastic Order is one of renunciation and must be understood as a forceful answer to the puzzle of the world. That there was a negative force impelling the youth to leave and renounce the world he knew is proved by his desire, three years later, to join the Carthusian Order and leave the Carmel in order to fulfill a destiny he saw then as one of absolute surrender of the self.

Three of the four years Juan de Santo Matía spent in Salamanca were devoted to his preparation for higher orders in the Carmel, which he received in the summer of 1567, thereby becoming a priest. A few weeks later he met Saint Theresa de Jesús at Medina del Campo and discussed with her the future of his religious life. The events of Salamanca are little known to us as far as they relate to the effect of university life on the young friar. He never mentioned these events or any others of his youth either in his writings, or, as far as we know, in his conversations with novices and students. Perhaps the desire of his contemporaries to remember only the edifying words and the doctrine he expounded exaggerates the monotony of his talks. Nevertheless, we must admit that in Saint John of the Cross renunciation was so complete that the recollection, and even more so, the relation of what had happened to him was not a normal part of his daily life. This trivial detail serves to picture the mature man better than long descriptions. His humility was so real that he never brought the details of his past to intrude into the consideration of ideas.

At a loss when faced with no first-hand knowledge, the historian has had to turn to the circumstantial evidence of the archives. As every friar, Juan de Santo Matía must have boarded at the Carmelite college in town, where masters of the Order taught courses. His name also appears in University records, and we know that he spent the years from 1564 to 1568 in Salamanca. We can then conjecture that he attended the classes all student-priests had to attend, since he is named with them as an *artista* first, a *teólogo* later. These words refer to the advancement in the career of all the students, not to any peculiar achievement of Juan de Santo Matía. About him in particular not much can be ascertained, although it is evident that he profited from his studies since he was trusted by his Order with the supervision of beginners both at the end of his stay in Salamanca and later in his life.

It is impossible even to ascertain what the young priest read or if he met in his years at Salamanca any of the great teachers we know were at the University then. Among them Fray Luis de León is the one history remembers best. He was an accomplished poet and a revered teacher, who was at this very moment engaged in a monumental struggle. He believed in the possibility of expressing the mysteries of religion in the language of the people, and had begun the translation of the "*Song of Songs*" into Spanish.

Fray Luis de León was among the forward-looking intellectuals of his times who were intent upon bringing to the common man the teachings and writings of the Church and the sacred books known to the clergy only in Latin. It is quite unlikely that Juan de Santo Matía could have lived in Salamanca and never have heard of the debate—over ten years old at this time—on the advantages of teaching in Spanish as opposed to the traditional Latin. In a sense his writings are part of this revolution that was bringing to the common people what had been the privilege of the few. In this respect there is a contradiction in Saint John's desire for a return to ancient rules of strict discipline and his liberalization of thought and democracy of language. These contradictions were part of his age: Spain was, in the European Renaissance, the country that tried most successfully to preserve the old and at the same time to introduce new ideas and new forms.

In both Salamanca and Medina del Campo there was great printing activity at this time. New forms of poetry, suppler, fuller, more attuned to the worldly aspirations of the age, were being tried. Instead of the popular song of charming brevity or the voluminous poems of didactic interest, a new Italianate verse of soft melodic lines and careful symmetry was tried at the beginning of the sixteenth century. And Fray Luis de León in Salamanca had tried to adapt the new forms to his lofty philosophical speculation—at times producing poems of proud

architectural beauty and even putting in the heroic lines of the
new metres the laments of an emotion of religious bereavement.
Saint John was not aware of all the varieties of literary life
around him. But he certainly must have read a few poems of the
new style—he even refers to such a stanzaic form on a unique
occasion when he discusses metrical innovations. His poetical
culture was, to be sure, haphazard, but his ear was faultless.

Perhaps something similar can be said about his acquaintance
with the theological and philosophical writings then in circulation.
His knowledge was haphazard, but his understanding was large.
There is evidence here and there of his acquaintance with the
religious thought of Northern Europe; there is some intimation
of the possibility that he knew Arabic mystics, but his biographers
insist only on his passionate reading of the Bible and of the
*Imitatio Christi* of Thomas à Kempis. This devotional breviary
had been translated and had become popular all over Europe
in the late fifteenth and early sixteenth century. It must have
guided Saint John in his daily devotions more than in his thinking.

There may have been many sources for Saint John's similes
of the mystic life. A great deal of his reasoning has ante-
cedents in treatises that were in the hands of all students
of theology. And yet, it is possible that Saint John never needed
the close study of the original sources. Was his mind of
such cast and power that his reflections and deductions supplied
all the necessary consequences to the bare ideas presented in
outlines and lectures? All his works reveal a close familiarity
with the Bible, almost the memorization of many parts of it.
But the interpretation and the fundamental doctrines he expounds seem to respond more to the teaching of the classroom
than to wide acquaintance with commentators. His doctrine
and his writings are more concerned with the world of experience
than with the world of books. In spite of what his relatives
and neighbors thought in Medina del Campo, the young priest
was not of a scholarly bent; when he left for Salamanca, he
did not intend to undertake the completion of a course of study.
He meant to enter the exercise of an exacting practice: that of
a man looking for the ultimate in renunciation.

IV  *The Turning Point*

The days of September of 1567 must have seemed to the

young priest one just as monotonous as any other. He was back in Medina del Campo on a vacation and due in Salamanca shortly to enter what was to be his last year of study. He probably spent many hours of each day looking out in the distance at the intense landscape of Castile, which blotted out every idea and every desire. The austerity of the plateau, its brown horizon, its loneliness was very much like his soul: monotonous and pure.

Was his life oriented towards the goal he desired? Had the University of Salamanca satisfied his curiosity? Perhaps in his mind he was convinced that nowhere on earth was there a place he wanted to occupy. What he needed most, he thought, was absolute silence. A way to live on as the bare sides of the mountains did, in solitary silence and uncomplaining resignation. And one day of September followed another, and the return to the disagreeable tumult and turmoil of the University was nearer at hand. Juan de Santo Matía did not know it then, but in one of these monotonous days of September his life was going to enter the realm of history. A conversation between him and Saint Theresa de Jesús, which she recorded, is the first document in which his mind is examined by other minds.

Saint Theresa's reform of the Carmelites was progressing. Her aim of restoring to the convents the old discipline lost in recent decades and her new ideas had not been received with approval. But the opposition had retreated, thanks to the help of a few powerful courtiers. King Philip II himself approved of a change in the Order, and the new Carmelites, who would later become a separate Order of Discalced Carmelites, were able to found a few convents for those nuns who wanted a life of stricter devotion. At this moment, Saint Theresa was looking for some priests of the Order of Carmel who desired a return to the old strict rules. Her nuns needed the help and guidance of confessors with the same desires for penance and contemplation. Some members of the Order suggested that this taciturn Friar Juan de Santo Matía might be interested.

From the testimony of Saint Theresa we know that Juan had the desire to leave the Carmel and enter the Carthusian Order. We also know that he was already secretly suffering penance and trying to lead a religious life more rigid and more strict than the Order required. Again, we have no way of finding out what forces, what thoughts, what experiences, convinced him, during his years as a student, or even before, during his work in the *Hospital de las Bubas*, to seek oblivion, solitude, and silence. For the Carthusian Order meant then, as it does today, a complete withdrawal, a vow of silence, and the constant and absolute attention to the inner search for perfection on the road to knowledge of God.

Saint Theresa prevailed on the youth. She convinced him it was possible, perhaps desirable, to serve in his own Order, even though he knew, he had to know, as well as she did, that this would be a less private and secluded service. They did not know, but they could at least dread the possibility of public suffering, disagreement, and displeasure. They could not, of course, foresee martyrdom—a fate that might have attracted them—but only the surrender of a private seclusion in what Juan de Santo Matía considered the happiness of silence in exchange for the uncertainties of a reform. Juan de Santo Matía accepted this new destiny, but not without exacting a condition: that he would not have to wait any longer than one year. Having exacted her promise that there would be a reformed monastery for men in less than a year, he returned to his theological studies at the University of Salamanca.

To Saint Theresa we owe also the only physical description of Saint John as he was at that moment. Saint Theresa, over twenty-five years older than Juan seems to have been struck with the young man's determination, but a little taken aback by his cold remoteness. There was some mockery in her description of the Carmelite friar as "half a friar"—he was short and emaciated. Perhaps there was also a wish to embrace and mother one who was so wise and mature for his age. Her admiration and respect for him grew with the years, yet he always showed the same remoteness that made him as a young man the sure choice for the spiritual direction of novices hardly any older than himself. His eyes seemed to have had a strange fixedness, his forehead was high, his hair thinning, his face bore the marks of penance and deprivation. There must have been a light in his eyes and a strange certainty in the tone of his voice, for nobody ever questioned his sincerity or his wisdom. Even when his enemies attacked and punished his body or slandered his character, they never questioned the precision of his serene intelligence.

It is clear that the young friar was determined to do something. As all young men who feel the call of greatness, he was to do something important—what it was he did not yet know—but he was certain to do it. And greatness for him was found in the humility of renunciation that led to knowledge and acceptance of the divine will. He seized his opportunity and made his decision, and, on November 20, 1568, took the vows of the Reformed Carmelites at Duruelo. With two other Carmelites, he established the first monastery of the Order in a modest house given to Saint Theresa by a well-wisher.

# CHAPTER 3

## The Carmelite Reform

*Qué bien sé yo la fonte que mana y corre,*
*Aunque es de noche.*
> *Cantar del alma que se huelga de*
> *conoscer a Dios por fe.*
(Well I know the fountain that runs and flows
Although it's night.
> Song of the soul that is glad to know
> God by faith.)

THE rules of the primitive Order of Carmel were simple and severe: the members elected a prior to whom they swore obedience; they attended Mass and prayed at appointed hours, and were enjoined to spend all their waking time at work or in meditation. Nothing could be owned as individuals by any of the brethren since all property became common property of the Order. The brethren abstained from eating meat, unless their health required it, and fasted at appointed times. There were also days set aside for them to meet and be chastised for any disobedience to the rules. By the sixteenth century a powerful and prosperous Order had developed from this simple origin. But the seed of decadence was visible when Saint Theresa started to worry about the Order. It did seem that its very success was destroying it. Not many of the friars were enthusiastic about missionary work in the Indies or about quiet meditation in solitude. At a moment when all of Europe was engaged in a fierce polemical battle on religious issues, and many priests were opposing the Protestant revolution with new fervor and new vigor, the friars and nuns of the Carmel seemed content just to enjoy their quiet comforts.

Only a few sisters had been willing to join Saint Theresa and up to this moment she could find no friars who were willing to give up the security of their well-appointed monasteries. Only one strange young man had thought for himself in the humility of his station and had decided to perform the duties of his

Order according to the old rules. He was fasting often and assigning extra duties and penances to himself without making a show of it. And, what was more important, he was teaching himself not to waste a single minute of his time; when not occupied with the necessary tasks of his daily life, he turned his mind to meditation upon the mysteries of knowledge and love.

At this moment of his life, Saint John was not, however, concerned with problems of doctrine or with clarification of his own religious experience. It is difficult to ascertain how much he had learned or thought about the new doctrines popular in Northern Europe or even about the threats of schism from groups within Spain. Certainly he must have heard about the *illuminati* who believed they could reach salvation through their own efforts, unaided by Church or priest; but even here we have no clear evidence to prove that the young friar had any notion of what role he might be called to play in the doctrinary affairs of his Church.

The most detailed study of his life at this moment gives us only the view of a man of almost unbelievable innocence. Those who had known him until then sensed a mystery in his steadfastness, but they directed Saint Theresa to him as a likely candidate for her venture mostly because they saw in him a different person, not conforming exactly to their idea of a successful priest in their town. Perhaps there was a touch of contempt for both the young friar and the novelties of a Discalced Reform in which few of them wanted to believe. Although two other priests were to join later, at this moment only one priest in the Order, Antonio de Heredia, showed interest in the venture, and he was, like Saint John, unique in the environment of the Carmel in Medina del Campo.

Antonio de Heredia was chosen to be the first of the new Order of Discalced Carmelites, and Saint John was willing to join him. In later accounts, and since Saint John had a prominent role in the affairs of the new Order, Antonio is thought of only as Saint John's companion. But nothing is farther from the truth. In 1567, when arrangements were made, and in 1568, when the two friars installed themselves in their new monastery, Antonio was the older and more experienced man. He was to be the Prior of the tiny Order.

Antonio de Heredia had also desired to join the Carthusians in his youth. Outwardly he was a man of delicate health and urbane manners, whose choice of the new way of life surprised everybody. He had risen in the Order and in 1567, already in his late fifties, he was Prior of the Monastery of Saint Ann in Medina. The priests in town, who shunned the company of the young Juan de Santo Matía, could understand his desire for a different life, but not their Prior's willingness to leave them for the hardships of a new and stricter religious life. Antonio de Jesús had an inner life, however, that they did not suspect. He was already preparing for his new duties, and had promised Saint Theresa that he would get together the few necessary items for the little monastery. He never thought of acquiring beds or cooking utensils, but he made sure that enough clocks— five of them, relates Saint Theresa—were available so that the new community would never miss its obligations and prayers.

Antonio de Jesús and Juan de la Cruz were to undertake the task of creating a new Order. For Saint John the task seems to have been only one of renunciation. At this time of his life, apparently, he was quite unaware of his own ability as a leader, and the position he was assigned as mentor of novices stemmed more from the circumstances around him than from his desires. Moreover, the first signs of a malady that was to be his companion for life, had already appeared. Little is known as to how this disease was contracted, and even as to what kind of disease it was. Saint John suffered from fevers and swellings in his limbs from his youth until his death.

He accepted his position with the same obedience he had shown as a child and which he had sworn to in his vows. In him humility was not the required virtue of his state, but a condition of his mind, and he felt in complete agreement with his fate, no matter where it led him. In the poverty of his chosen vocation, he felt he was strengthening his faith and atoning for the sins and vices the flesh of man is heir to. He must have believed then that his life of silence was to be a quiet offering to God unnoticed by society. Yet he was not to die an unknown man. Others were to come and seek him out to persecute or worship him, and, one day, he himself was to live through an experience he felt had to be shared with everybody else.

## I  *The House at Duruelo*

Besides Antonio de Jesús and John of the Cross, a third priest, José de Cristo, of whom little is known, came to the new monastery. A fourth Carmelite joined them at the beginning, but nothing is known about him. Since he is said to have been old and infirm, we may assume he returned to the mitigated Order after finding the new rigors too harsh for him.

Saint Theresa had been offered a small house in Duruelo, some twenty miles from Avila on the road to Medina del Campo. Duruelo was a hamlet of barely twenty houses. The house given to the Carmelites to be used as their first monastery for men had been used by a bailiff for the storage of grain, which he received as rents. It was very small, really only one room divided into two with a porch and a loft. When in June of 1568 Saint Theresa and her companions inspected it, they found it completely inadequate, but decided it would have to do: the porch was to be converted into a church, and the room below was to serve as bedroom for the friars.

Prior to the foundation of the new house, John of the Cross was given a temporary assignment in Valladolid, where he helped Saint Theresa with the founding of a convent and the instruction of the novice nuns during the summer months. At the end of September he went to Duruelo to work on the farmhouse in anticipation of its occupancy. Although he was ill most of the period, he did what he could all by himself until the 28th of November, when Antonio de Jesús and José de Cristo joined him. "The porch was transformed into a chapel, decorated with crosses made from branches of trees; the garret had become the choir; the dwelling-room a dormitory of two cells, each with its little window looking towards the altar, and its bed of straw with a stone for pillow; part of the kitchen had been cut off for a refectory, in which a block of wood stood as table, a broken pitcher and two gourdshells forming the dinner service."[1]

In spite of John's efforts, the roof still leaked. Rain, sleet, and snow found their way to the Carmelites' beds. They slept little. They ate what was given to them in the town, which was itself quite poor. They wore habits of coarse serge, and in accordance with their rules, which were changed some twenty years later to permit them to wear sandals, went barefooted. In this way they were distinguished from the regular Carmelites of the Observance who wore shoes and whose habits were made of regular cloth. Neither branch of the Order lived in wealth or comfort, but the Discalced or Reformed Carmelites disdained even the most elementary needs. They were interested only in their faith.

The friars of the new Order attracted the attention of people in town and in the surrounding countryside. Very soon converts called on them and wanted to join their life of penance. Again John of the Cross was chosen to instruct them, perhaps because of his persuasive and commanding humility. There was something arresting in his firmness. The newcomer was not put off by the harshness of his exacting nature because he never asked more of others than of himself. Saint John was trusted because he did not command by the rule, but by his own example.

For almost two years, the pale young man lived in the austerity of this farmhouse in Duruelo. Success for him, and for his mentor Saint Theresa, was clear in the peace of this community. There were now some twenty novices and never a complaint. John instructed them in obedience and in the joys of meditation and prayer. They were only too willing to obey their Prior, Antonio de Jesús, who in his old age, and after having advanced to high position, was willing and happy to retire to the oblivion of a life of penance in this remote farmhouse.

For John of the Cross there was need of nothing more. He chastised his body only to make sure that nothing would take his mind from his aim. He had arranged for the corners of the Church in the old porch to be turned into two little hermitages for friar Antonio and himself. Since the roof was too low, Antonio and John had to sit or lie down to say their prayers in them. Two stones served as pillows, and above these they placed crosses and skulls to remind themselves of the proximity of death. They prayed their matins long before dawn and remained there until daybreak. Sometimes they would be so engrossed in their meditation that their habits would be covered with the snow that fell through the open windows without their noticing it.

The three priests—and later their disciples—used to go out and preach in many places in the district. Since there were no other monasteries in the vicinity, their spiritual advice, their teaching, and their good offices in caring for the sick were welcome. They soon acquired a good reputation and became loved by the humble peasants of the region. They went out as far as they could reach on foot, through the wind and snow, and returned late at night, after preaching and hearing confessions. They found their new life happy and absorbing because they had but one desire: to give of themselves.

Soon the gentlemen who lived in neighboring villages began to help the industrious friars of Duruelo with gifts of food and furnishings. One of them had had a church built in a place called Mancera, a few miles from Duruelo, to enshrine a picture of Our Lady that his parents had brought from the Low Countries. He offered the church as a monastery for the Discalced Carmelites, who decided to transfer their house from Duruelo, since the new Church offered the rooms necessary for the growing community. Neither Antonio de Jesús nor Juan de la Cruz ever forgot the humble farmhouse in which they had begun a new life, and often they returned in their memories to these days of almost absolute poverty. In the midst of the trials and tribulations that success was to bring to their undertaking, the house of Duruelo was remembered as an abode of peace and quiet happiness.

## II  *Saint John as Spiritual Director*

The year of 1568 that saw the beginning of a new spirituality within the Order of the Carmel was also the year the beliefs of the *illuminati* were condemned as heretical for the first time. What seemed to John of the Cross and his mother a peaceful resolution of their many family problems was only a breathing spell. Catalina Alvarez had joined the little group as cook and general helper. Francisco de Yepes and his wife were also attached to the monastery at Duruelo, and later to the house at Mancera. Francisco, in his position of lay brother, used to walk with John and listen to his preaching. They partook of frugal meals. John rejected invitations to sumptuous or at least hearty dinners, not out of disdain for the peasants, but out of humility and in order to keep the light of thought and meditation burning.

There was a quiet joy in the mortification of the flesh that made the tiny community different from large monasteries. The rules of the new Order made necessary common understanding and good will. John was the most fervent of the brethren. It is related that once, after having asked for supper a little earlier than usual because he was ill, he repented of this hasty surrender to the body and accused himself in front of the community. He lashed his back in punishment while the other friars looked on.

But the routine of Duruelo and Mancera was not one of harshness and self-punishment. The friars liked to walk in the countryside, and they sang as they walked. John of the Cross, as well as Saint Theresa, believed in the possibility of faith and good works without gloom. Saint Theresa visited the House of Duruelo in March of 1569 and admired the high spirits of the priests, especially of the aging Antonio de Jesús.

After the move to Mancera in June of 1570, Saint John was to have some five months of peace left. In late October or early November he was called to Pastrana to become the teacher of fourteen new priests in what was to be the second house of the Reformed Order. Francisco went with him in the hope that life in Pastrana, some forty miles from Madrid, would be similar to their calling at Mancera. But the Order had need of more instruction. Saint Theresa felt that the state of religious life in Spain called for fervor and study. The simplicity of peasant devotion was no longer enough. And with the creation of a Carmelite College in Alcalá de Henares, near Madrid, Saint John entered a different period of his life. He was sent there as the director of this first school of Discalced Carmelites.

Saint John was chosen no doubt not only because of his university training at Salamanca, but also because of his personal traits that made him the best counsellor to the aspiring monks. In Alcalá, a university founded in 1508 in imitation of La Sorbonne, the students of the Order attended lectures in theology in the common classrooms but lived in a Carmelite House and were under the direction of John of the Cross. As adviser and tutor John could not escape the influence of the University itself. There were then courses in theology, philosophy, and medicine, together with mathematics, rhetoric, Greek and Hebrew, and letters. Could he live for fourteen months in close contact with the students and not hear some echoes of the myriad subjects and disputes of the classroom? We have no records or witnesses to his learning, but John's own words, the adage that his students learned to revere, explain to us both his learning, which was vast, and the impossibility we find of pinpointing its origins:

*Religioso y estudiante, y el religioso delante.*

"A religious and a student, and first religious," he repeated in sententious brevity. But the rhyme in this maxim was childish, without any notion yet of the skill in the use of sounds in his later verse. Saint John the poet had not yet been born.

After some further travel, including a short sojourn in Pastrana, Saint John was called to take charge of the spiritual direction of the 130 nuns of the Convent of the Incarnation in Avila in September of 1572. This was the convent in which Saint Theresa had been a novice and a nun long before she had decided to reform the Order. It had been here where, after the death of her father, she had fallen ill and had heard a voice that bade her set forth on her incredible undertaking. Since then she had founded many convents, and the future of her project seemed assured. The house she had left needed her now.

The Convent of Carmelites in Avila had been the scene of scandalous behavior. Nuns were leading a life almost as free as townspeople, receiving visitors and enjoying dances and music. Some gentlemen in town were so bold as to claim the affections of some of the nuns, who were enjoying a kind of love game. When Saint Theresa was brought to take charge of the Convent of the Incarnation, many of the nuns feared the changes she would bring and openly opposed her. She succeeded, nevertheless, in winning most of them to her side. Both she, as their prioress, and John of the Cross, as their spiritual director, proceeded with infinite patience in bringing to them the reform they had feared.

A small house was built near the convent for John of the Cross and his helpers. The nuns brought to him his frugal meals, and he heard their confessions and guided them on the painful road of renunciation. It was perhaps in this convent of Avila, where John of the Cross spent five years of quiet and purposeful work, that he first saw the way of contemplation give fruit. We have, though, no writings of this period. It is safe to assume that, had the world been content to let John of the Cross instruct these 130 nuns, there would have been no history: he would have lived and died in the normal and uneventful monotony of a convent of the sixteenth century, in which the rare rebellion of a nun, struck by madness or driven to suicide, was the only interruption in a round of prayers, confessions, masses, more confessions and prayers. Friar John heard confessions once a week, or at least every other week, listened to every one of them with thoughtful patience, and had for each of the nuns words of encouragement and advice. He knew every one of them for he considered each a special soul given to him to lead.

By 1577 the Carmelites of the Observance had become suspicious of their new Reformed brethren. They were envious, perhaps, of their success in the Convent of the Incarnation and wanted to regain their old quarters. At a famous election in October of 1577, they had hoped to unseat Saint Theresa, but the results were overwhelmingly in her favor, and they were furious. They were well aware that the success of the Convent owed much to the work of John of the Cross and Germán de San Matías, who was living with him, and decided to abduct them. They captured the two friars and took them to their convent in Avila, and from there they transferred Germán to La Moraleja and John to Toledo. Germán was able to escape in a few days; but John of the Cross could not escape, and all of the efforts of Saint Theresa, who even pleaded with the King to interfere, were of no avail. Saint John spent almost nine months as a prisoner of the Carmelites in their convent in Toledo, some forty-five miles south of Madrid.

### III  *In Prison in Toledo*

In Toledo, Friar John of the Cross was imprisoned in a cell of some six by ten feet, without any windows and with only a small skylight by which he had to read his prayer book following a niggardly ray of sun. His door was kept locked, and he was allowed to go out of the cell only once a day, accompanied by the guard who watched his cell constantly.

It is not easy, after four centuries, to understand the web of circumstances that brought about the imprisonment of Friar John of the Cross. In addition to the passage of time, which has obscured the conflict of principles involved and cast into oblivion the reasons behind petty jealousies and envy, there has been a traditional evaluation of the event which has completely obliterated facts and reason to give vent to emotional partisanship. "It is undeniable, in any case, and this suffices for our information, that his enemies saw in John of the Cross a dangerous being, whose influence it was judged necessary to

counteract."² The legal complexity of the affair can be summarized briefly. The Carmelites of the Observance considered
that the house John and his helper Germán de San Matías
occupied was a third monastery, besides Mancera and Pastrana,
in violation of the authorization to found only two monasteries
given to the Discalced Carmelites. Saint John was made prior
of Mancera to forestall the imprisonment, but the appointment
came too late.

It is quite understandable that, after Saint John's innocence
had been proved, his followers should turn in accusation against
his enemies. Again, facts are further obscured by accusations and
counter-accusations. We cannot judge Saint John's enemies by
counter-accusations any more than we can judge Saint John by
the accusations of his enemies. Apparently, accusations against
Saint John were of such monstrous nature that biographers have
not dared to repeat them.

Accusations of this kind would not explain the personal
animosity shown in the treatment of Friar John of the Cross by
his brothers of the Observance during his imprisonment. They
were the basis, however, for repeated trials during and after his
life by the competent tribunals of the Church, out of which the
works of Saint John have emerged as orthodox and consistent
with the doctrines of the Catholic Church. We should look
elsewhere for an explanation, for instance, of the circular
discipline, a form of punishment in the Carmelite prisons. In
this form of torture, every one of the monks was forced to flog
the prisoner in turn, until the whole community satisfied its
curiosity in seeing his suffering and had the dubious pleasure of
contributing to it. Indeed there must have been a general disease
of the mind that required flagellation. Even worse, as proved
by an incident in one of the monasteries directed by Saint John
himself, public flagellation could be cherished by some as a form
of penance.

At one time, Friar John of the Cross had left the monastery
in Pastrana in the charge of a young priest, Angel de San Gabriel.
On his return, he found to his dismay that the monks had been
obliged to flagellate themselves in the public square for the
whole town to witness and enjoy the spectacle. It is no wonder
that in an atmosphere of such relish for corporal punishments,
the circular discipline was applied without hesitation. No one

could see anything wrong with it. If we add that some monks had suffered reprimands and other punishments when John had been their superior, we might also suspect some personal reasons for dislike and even hatred in the repeated tortures he underwent in the nearly nine months he spent in a cell in Toledo.

In his own mind, however, none of the tortures his brothers of the Observance could devise was significant. John of the Cross had schooled his body in penitence and self-punishment, and he could accept this treatment as one more step towards the attainment of his goal. The torture of his body was joy for him because he knew that this pain was required for perfection. Even the insults heaped on him by the torturing monks were or could be further proof of the love of a God who had decreed that suffering purifies.

The routine of the cell, day in and day out, was simple. The few hours in which the sun filtered through a small window were devoted to reading the breviary. Once a day he was taken to a larger room where he would eat bread and drink water and, occasionally, he was given a few sardines. Exercise and the needs of the body were taken care of in this daily period also. In the evening the prisoner was taken out—at least once a week— to be offered complete pardon if he abjured his rebellious reform. He was even offered the post of prior of a regular monastery. After his steadfast refusal was answered with taunts and insults, he was ordered to lift his habit—he was forced to wear the cloth of the Observance—and he was lashed by everyone present.

It was difficult not to fall into temptation. Not, as the other friars thought, into the temptation of renouncing his beliefs, but into a subtler temptation known only to Saint John's innermost thoughts. He could not help trembling each time he was given some food: was it poisoned or was his mind befouled by calumny? Was he in the right or were his fears a cloud of unreason designed to tempt his soul?

Only when he could return to the darkness and the loneliness of his cell, could Saint John forget his torture. There were strange moments of blissful rapture in the midst of his sufferings. A light that did not hurt his eyes or the ringing of caressing words that repeated a few lines were part of his hallucinatory prison:

*Qué bien sé yo la fonte que mana y corre,*
*Aunque es de noche.*

          *Cantar del alma que se huelga*
           *de conoscer a Dios por fe.*

(Well I know the fountain that runs and flows
Although it's night.

          Song of the soul that is glad
           to know God by faith.)

In the unbearable cold and dampness, his thought was like fire
and light. And there was the warmth of consolation in a presence
that transfigured the night when he spoke:

ESPOSA

    *¿A dónde te escondiste,*
*Amado, y me dejaste con gemido?*
*Como el ciervo huiste,*
*Habiéndome herido;*
*Salí tras ti clamando, y eras ido.*
    *Pastores los que fuerdes*
*Allá por las majadas al otero,*
*Si por ventura vierdes*
*Aquel que yo más quiero,*
*Decidle que adolezco, peno y muero.*
    *Buscando mis amores,*
*Iré por esos montes y riberas,*
*Ni cogeré las flores,*
*Ni temeré las fieras,*
*Y pasaré los fuertes y fronteras.*

(BRIDE

    Where are you hiding,
Beloved, having left me to moan?
Like the stag you fled
After wounding me;
I followed crying aloud, but you had gone.
    Shepherds, you that go
Through the sheepfolds to the hills,
If by chance you see
Him that I love most,
Tell him that I suffer, grieve, and die.
    Searching for my love
I will wander amongst mountains and rivers,

I will not gather flowers
Nor fear the prowling beasts,
And I will pass through all the forts and frontiers.)

The lines he heard seemed not to follow one another for a while. But rhyme and sense required certain arrangements, and he tried again and again to recall the lines in a logical sequence, until his memory was no longer able to hold all he had dreamed or thought. It is said that he asked of a jailer a notebook and ink, and jotted down the lines that came to him, without knowing that he would spend the rest of his life completing, annotating, and commenting upon them.

### IV   *Escape from Prison*

John of the Cross could endure all these sufferings. But being deprived of the consolation of his religious duties was beyond thought. It is perhaps in protest against this injustice that he decided to escape, although there must have been a cruel moment of hesitation between his desire to keep his vows of obedience and the need to say Mass once again.

John's escape was not easy. His new jailer, Juan de Santa María, took pity on him, it is true. The jailer recalled years afterwards how he had been awed by the stony silence of the little friar, when every one of the Carmelites added insult to the whip and threats to the insults. But it is unlikely that John found any help in him. The very fear of punishment must have kept his guardians from it, since, according to the Carmelite rule, the guardian would have to replace the prisoner if he let him escape.

Apparently, John of the Cross had studied the lock on his door carefully, and had managed to loosen it a little at a time. One night he decided it was time to take it out in order to open the door. His vows of obedience to the Order required him to stay and suffer whatever punishment the Order thought he deserved. His own beliefs, his desires for perfection and humility, should have rejoiced at the opportunity to suffer immensely and even t die in his cell. He must have hesitated for a long moment. His sufferings were beyond belief and almost beyond endurance, and yet he had received the clearest signs of grace in that tiny cell from which he felt he had to escape.

Either in his memory or in a small notebook—we shall never know for sure—he had stored many stanzas of incomplete poems that spoke of the consolation of a truth and a light that shines in the darkest of nights. Could he expect the same light to shine again in the light of everyday? Were that light and that fountain to be lost if he left the darkness of his torture?

Later in his life John of the Cross was to avow that years of imprisonment could not be sufficient payment for the bliss he experienced in the solitary night of this confinement. Yet he knew he had to escape if he wanted to say Mass again. Perhaps he wanted also to bring to the words he remembered and repeated the full life of being heard and read. He must have known there was something he had to say, for it is after his escape that he becomes a writer, in prose and in verse, with an energy akin to fury.

As he walked out of his cell into the common room of the convent, he heard the heavy breathing of two friars asleep on the floor. He had to tiptoe to the opposite end of the big room without awakening them. One of the friars seemed startled for a fraction of a second; John held his breath. No sounds in the night; he had reached the window safely. The wood was so rotten it might have given away even under his slight weight. He had to be careful, slide out of the window almost without touching it. In preparation he made a long rope by tearing and knotting together strips of his blankets, and, with their help, he slid down. He had miscalculated. There were a few feet left for him to jump. He landed in the yard unhurt. A dog heard the fall, but did not bark. It was dark, and John did not know the way out—he was still far from freedom.

John frightened the dog by throwing rocks at him, and ran in the direction of the dog's escape, hoping to find the way. Suddenly he was in the streets of a city he did not know in the darkest hour of the night, just before dawn, not knowing if he had been followed or not. He walked aimlessly for a while, then at daybreak he called at a house and asked how to reach the Convent of Discalced Carmelites. Once here, the sisters marveled to see him and found a hiding place in the infirmary where he confessed a gravely ill nun. When the Carmelites of the Observance called at the Convent, searching for him, they never thought of looking into the forbidden rooms, where only confessors could enter.

The joyful nuns brought to John of the Cross some baked pears to restore his strength, and John of the Cross took heart. In the quiet of the nunnery he recited to the enraptured nuns the stanzas of his "Spiritual Canticle." They listened and were thrilled. They believed as he did in the reality of the words they were hearing. For them and for him they spoke not only with the beauty of rhythm and sense but with a truth beyond the tangible world. John of the Cross had found the words that told with perfect accuracy the experience about which he had spoken in his teaching as spiritual adviser. From this moment on, his life was to be devoted almost entirely to the explanation of this revelation. In the few months spent in the prison of Toledo he had acquired the absolute value of an experience never to be repeated. In the darkness of his suffering he had discovered the words and the symbols with which he could express the innermost desires of his soul.

# CHAPTER 4

## The Reform Succeeds

*El más puro padecer, trae y acarrea
más puro entender.*
*Avisos y sentencias*

(Suffering in purity brings about
and produces a purer knowledge.
Spiritual Maxims, Instructions
and Preaching)

WHILE the nuns copied and rejoiced and asked questions, John of the Cross remembered and recited or read out of the little book he had brought with him from his prison. But the Prioress had a practical turn of mind. She saw the dangers of the situation and wrote to the most powerful friend of the Discalced Carmelites in the city of Toledo, Don Pedro González de Mendoza, a wealthy gentleman who was the director of the Hospital of the Holy Cross and a canon and treasurer of the Church of Toledo. She asked him to come to them with armed servants to protect friar John of the Cross. For the following weeks, Saint John was given protection and asylum in the Hospital of the Holy Cross. He rested here, trying to recover his strength and dwelling on the memories of his dreadful days in prison, for which he thanked and blessed the Carmelites of the Observance, since they had brought to him the sweetness of poetic rapture and the delights of new words.

In October of that year of 1578, the Reform held a meeting in Almodóvar del Campo, not far from Toledo. Friar Antonio de Jesús, the former prior at Duruelo, had convened this Chapter meeting to deal with pressing problems of the Order. In the preceding weeks the Papal Nuncio had ordered the imprisonment of high officers of the Discalced Carmelites and had deprived their Provincial, Father Gracián, of his powers. The Reform was in danger of extinction. It was felt that the presence of John of the Cross was necessary, both because of his long experience in administration and spiritual advice and because of his new importance as a source of contention between the Reform and the Old Order. Fortunately Don Pedro González could assure him safe transport, providing him with a coach and the protection of his servants.

When he arrived in Almodóvar, he found that the two possible courses of action for the Chapter were the immediate institution of the Reform as a separate Order in defiance of the Nuncio, or submission to the Carmelites of the Observance and appeal to the Pope. In accordance with the meekness of his soul and the vows of obedience he wanted so much to keep, John advocated submission. Perhaps there was in him a desire for more suffering and a hope of obtaining greater depth. But his counsel did not prevail: an attempt was made to separate the Reform from the Observance, Father Antonio was elected Provincial, and two friars were commissioned to go to Rome to present the Chapter's views to the Pope and obtain approval of its daring actions.

One of the emissaries was the prior of the Monastery of El Calvario, in northern Andalusia in the mountains of Segura. The Chapter elected Saint John to replace him while he went to Rome and also instructed him to visit the Convent of Beas on his way to El Calvario in order to help the nuns there with their spiritual problems.

Saint John had not been too successful in the meetings at Almodóvar; he was not meant for high office or political power. There was perhaps a touch of contempt in the general reception of his meek proposals of submission to the Carmelites of the Observance, and the position to which he was sent was not certainly among the highest in the Order. In spite of Saint John's recent suffering and steadfast loyalty, there might also have been some antagonism among his brethren. Little did they think that no place could have been more welcome to his aspirations than this exile in the mountains of Andalusia.

The peaceful setting of El Calvario was a needed refuge to Saint John's tired soul and indefatigable mind. Within the precincts of this monastery, there was a hill in which streams, fountains, and waterfalls provided the running sound of water he loved so much to hear. There were caves, rocks, and trees providing solitude where he could hide and meditate in absolute quiet. Before taking up his new position, however, as we have indicated, he spent a few weeks at the Convent of Beas, as confessor and spiritual director of the nuns. Their questions prompted him to begin a line by line commentary of his "Spiritual Canticle." In this way their request and his solitude conspired to give form to a treatise in which he could expound his doctrine.

These attempts were a novelty for Saint John. He had a body of lines that carried a great deal of meaning to him. But he was never sure that the listeners could penetrate every metaphor, expand every suggestion. Since his poetry often echoed passages of his readings in the Bible, there was the need of recalling the passage to the novices. Also, the spiritual meaning of the whole could be subverted by attention to a detail or through misconstruction of a word or sentence. The best way to bring understanding of the poems seemed then to be a careful reading and explanation of each line, preceded by a declaration concerning the intention of the whole poem or stanza. The work he was to undertake might have seemed pleasant and easy at the beginning, but soon John found that explanation of a verse led into considerations of doctrine, and his treatises became the exposition of his thought and the guide to the way of contemplation rather than the line-by-line clarification of difficulties in his verse. In this way, the writings of Saint John became two distinct bodies—one in verse, one in prose—intimately related, but independently valid in the history of literature and the evolution of religious thought.

When John of the Cross settled in El Calvario, he did not forget his duties towards the nuns of Beas. Every Saturday he would make the long walk—in about two or three hours—to their convent to give them the consolation of confession and of his inspired talks. He would spend the weekends in Beas and return to El Calvario to assume his duties on Mondays.

His weekend talks dealt with passages of his own poems. He had to explain to the nuns the way his lines responded to experiences of his own, the way they reflected and rewove his reading of the Bible and his knowledge of theology, and also how they could be used as a tool for meditations on the pleasures of the contemplative life and the delights to be bestowed on the soul that seeks perfection. After his oral explanation, the thoughts of the preceding weekend must have haunted·him for a few days, and the anticipation of explanation to come on the next Sunday must have brought a kindling of enthusiasm and a fever of words to his lips. He had no choice but to give all of his thoughts some form in writing. Perhaps it was during this period that he composed, together with the treatise on the "Spiritual Canticle," at least part of the *Ascent to Mount Carmel*, a commentary on a poem of the same title.

Saint John spent nearly a year of quiet and continuous work in El Calvario and Beas. The Guadalquivir River, the sweet vegetation of Andalusia, the clear sky, and the solitude made life in this humble residence a joy, although we know he missed his native Castile and felt nostalgia for its barren landscape. But the affairs of the Order were to require more sacrifices of him. He was directed to proceed to the town of Baeza—some miles south—to found a convent in June of 1579, and there he spent a few months before attending a meeting of the Discalced Carmelites in March of 1580 in Alcalá de Henares.

The affairs of the Reform had prospered. The Carmelites had been forced to accept the Discalced branch as a separate province of the Order. The deliberations of the friars now were not clouded over by apprehension and fear. They discussed their affairs and proceeded to hold elections in an atmosphere of understanding and great hope. Saint John himself had an important role in the deliberations and was more warmly accepted than ever before. He was elected Third Definitor, a position of no great authority, to be sure, but one of prestige and importance. His superior ability to instruct and advise was indeed amply acknowledged, since he was elected Rector of the Carmelite College of Baeza for the following two years.

The years he spent in this town of Baeza were fruitful to his writing and thinking. He was busy also with numerous duties in the College and as advisor to the nuns. From time to time, his energies were taxed with unexpected tasks, as, for instance, during a strange epidemic of fevers and coughing that hit the city in 1580. His old sickness returned again and again and made his daily tasks more difficult and painful. Yet, on the whole, the uneventful days of hard work left enough serenity and a few hours once in a while to return to the manuscripts which he was preparing for the edification of the nuns who were entrusted to his direction. This task was for him only a kind of solace, since

Saint John felt neither the desire for publication nor the ambition to rival literary artificers or theological thinkers with his verse or his prose.

## I  *In the Hierarchy of the Reform*

The duties of Saint John in Baeza were not very different from the duties he had discharged nine years before in the College of Alcalá. In both places, neighboring universities provided the courses in many fields of knowledge needed by the novices, while the Rector of the College was in charge of their spiritual well-being and was constantly watching over their progress in the paths of meditation and devotion to their calling. Saint John participated also in their learned disputes and was always called upon to help them resolve their doubts.

Towards the end of the year of 1581, the Order decided to change the duties of the Rector of the College. He was then given the task of Prior of the Convent of the Martyrs in Granada, in Southern Spain, and almost simultaneously he was requested to proceed to the foundation of a new convent of discalced nuns in the same city of Granada. Although he still longed for a return to Castile, John of the Cross accepted with obedient happiness his new tasks. He travelled to Avila, where he spent nearly a month, to consult with Saint Theresa, and, on his return, effected the foundation of the Convent in June of 1582. Meanwhile he had taken up his post as Prior of Los Mártires either at the end of 1581 or at the beginning of 1582.

Los Mártires is located very near the famous gardens of the Generalife in the Alhambra. The haunting beauty of the spacious gardens and the entrancing sounds of the Moorish fountains delighted the friars and the occasional visitor in those days as they delight the numerous visitors today. At dusk or at night, the mystery of the gardens and the babbling waters seduce like a charm, while, in the light of the sun, the color and the richness of the vegetation are like an opiate to all thoughts of worldly interests. "The effect of moonlight, too, on the Alhambra has something like enchantment. Every rent and chasm of time, every mouldering tine and weather stain disappears; the marble resumes its original whiteness, the long colonnades brighten in the moon beams; the halls are illuminated with a softened radiance, until the whole edifice reminds one of the enchanted palace of an Arabian tale . . . The peculiar charm of this old dreamy palace, is its power of calling up vague reveries and picturings of the past, and thus clothing naked realities with the illusions of the memory and the imagination . . . Here the hand of time has fallen the lightest, and the traces of Moorish elegance and splendour exist in almost their original brilliancy . . . Every thing here appears calculated to inspire kind and happy feelings, for every thing is delicate and beautiful. The very light falls tenderly from above, through the lantern of a dome tinted and wrought as if by fairy hands."[1]

Adding to the enchantment of the new place for John of the Cross was the arrival of Francisco, his brother, who was able to join him here, and everything seemed to be in place. The next years, in fact almost seven years, were calmly spent in the routine of well-loved work. But the first year of John's administration was disturbed by a raging epidemic of what appears to have been bubonic plague. Saint John himself was ill for three days with high fever and incipient buboes which fortunately healed soon. And yet, the threat was always there: illness, fevers, and epidemics of many kinds were always near.

Even when in health, the life of the Prior in Granada was not leisurely. To the affairs of his own monastery were added the tasks of spiritual direction of the nuns of the new convent. His fame as a counselor, moreover, had spread in town, and many laymen came to him to hear his words and, often, to confess and to enter more definitely into a life of contemplation and detachment. Incredible as it may seem to us today, John of the Cross could find time for all of his duties. Never did he turn away a sincere soul asking for help, and his leisure was occupied with the perfecton of yet another treatise or the correction of the writings he had completed in El Calvario.

The last of Saint John's important books, *La Llama de amor viva (Living Flame of Love)*, was probably written in Granada. This theological treatise is, as the three preceding it, an extended commentary on a poem with the same title. The poem "Living Flame of Love" must also have been written in Granada and was the last poem written by Saint John. It is, indeed, a fitting crown to a flight of inspiration that soared to the highest possibilities of expression in language and then went silent as though further words were no longer necessary or possible.

In the years from 1582 to 1588, Saint John's time was spent in Granada, except for travelling connected with affairs of the Order and a brief period when he was the Vicar Provincial of Andalusia and had to visit periodically all the houses of the Order. Among his most taxing activities was the attendance at meetings of the Reform in which important decisions were made. In the spring of 1583, for instance, he tried to convince his brethren in a Chapter meeting at Almodóvar that no foreign missions should be undertaken by the Reformed Carmelites. He also wanted to change the rules for the election of priors to make it impossible for them to be reelected. The Order rejected the ideas of Saint John, and missionaries were sent to foreign lands. At the same time, his brethren refused to bow to his desires, and reelected him Prior of Granada, in this way showing both their great respect and admiration for his accomplishment, but refusing to imitate him to the full extent of his renunciation of the affairs of this world.

In 1588, the Order decided again to transfer John of the Cross, this time to Segovia, a town of Old Castile, some fifty miles northwest of Madrid. The seat of the Order had been transferred to this city to avoid the influence of the capital, with its distractions and political dissensions. And John was to be in charge of all preparations for a major meeting. He continued his life of ascetic detachment, interrupted for a few days by the visit of his brother Francisco, who always brought to him great consolation. Unfortunately, this visit in Segovia was to be the last days of some enjoyment in the life of Saint John. New trials were in store for him. Soon after Francisco left, he received the sad news of the death of his mother, Catalina de Alvarez, who had become a Carmelite nun taking the name of Mary of the Incarnation. And at the ensuing meeting of the Chapter, he was to suffer again the persecutions that misunderstanding and envy prepare for the unwary.

## II  *A New Persecution*

Saint John had occupied some of the highest positions in the affairs of his Order. Not only had his authority been great at times, but he had also obtained the success of intellectual recognition. Begrudgingly, perhaps even by mistake, he had been granted the necessary peace and solitude to continue with his inner work and to devote endless hours to silent meditation. His spirit had never succumbed to temptation, and his strength was not directed towards the desire of greater accomplishment or more powerful positions. On the contrary, his brother Francisco has related that, at about this time, when he visited him in Segovia, Saint John told him of a vision in which he had been asked what reward he desired for his suffering and his work. John had answered a painting of Christ that seemed to speak to him that he only wanted to suffer more deeply and to be persecuted for the love he felt.

Now while he was living in Segovia, it seemed that his wishes were about to come true. His meditation and prayers had become so ethereal that even writing about them was unnecessary, and, after adding a few touches to his prior work and writing a few poetic lines, Saint John ceased to try. There were letters that had to be sent; the affairs of the Order had to be looked after; new Chapters were scheduled to meet. But all of these obstacles were easily forgotten. He could look back on a long life of suffering, remembering only the sweet moments of silent thought. His humble mother had died serenely in old age, and the moving spirit of the Reform, Saint Theresa herself, had died. Through them he had learned how to die. Nothing held him to the world. His peace was complete. Undoubtedly, as a twentieth-century thinker conjectures, this period of his life holds the secret of mystical surrender of the self and a peace that is beyond understanding.[2]

Early in the year of 1590, some discalced nuns had obtained directly from the Pope the authorization to have their affairs separated from the general affairs of the Order and dependent on a special appointee of the Vicar General. Anne of Jesus, Prioress of Beas, had been the leading force in this movement for independence. It was well known that she was a favorite disciple of John of the Cross. She herself had requested his appointment as their confessor, and so, although Saint John had not had any direct part in Anne's requests, he was thought of as her ally. He himself believed sincerely that the nuns should have more freedom and that that was the way Saint Theresa would have wanted the convents she had founded to be governed. In this he was seconded only by Friar Luis de León, the old teacher of Salamanca, who was present at the meetings held in Madrid in

1590. At least three generations of reformers were meeting here, the older nuns who had known Saint Theresa well when she had been young and who were now taking mostly an advisory position in the affairs of the Order; the men who had followed Saint Theresa and were now governing the Order—except for John of the Cross whose voice was heard but who had little authority now; and a younger generation already confused about the beginnings of the Reform and the aims of Saint Theresa. The nuns were rebuffed again and again, and John of the Cross began to feel the oppressive hand of fate.

In June of 1591, an important meeting took place in Madrid. When elections were held, John received no office. He rejoiced at this new deprivation that returned him to the humble position of simple discalced friar. Since the antagonism among his peers was great, he decided to look for a distant place where they would forget him. The new governing body accepted his offer to go to New Spain with twelve Carmelite friars in a missionary expedition. Perhaps John dreamed for a moment of the distant lands of Mexico, of new stars and new emotions in the silent meditations during long nights of solitude. But it was to be only a dream. He was sent to the Monastery of La Peñuela near Ubeda in the province of Jaén in northern Andalusia in preparation for the journey, or so he thought, while the authorities of the Order studied his future.

While he fasted and prayed in retirement, the news reached him that some of the high dignitaries of the Order were planning his downfall. They had commanded that a member of the Order should travel through the monasteries John had lived in gathering information about his activities. The witnesses were tricked, bribed, or forced into strange accusations in the hope of expelling John from the Order.

When Saint John learned of the intentions of his enemies and was asked to defend himself in writing, he refused to do so. He answered all good friends that it was impossible that he shoud be expelled from the Order, since he was ready to obey no matter what he might be asked to do. And his only desire was to continue to live and to suffer as a member of the Carmelite Order. His officious enemies continued to coerce and convince nuns and priests to sign affidavits expounding supposed crimes and petty offenses. But yet he knew in his painful solitude that he would obey and suffer any punishment rather than give up his vocation. It must have been a great consolation to him to know that he had within him the fortitude to endure the most ignominious torture, the pain of prison, the constant physical punishment, and the spiritual sufferings he had already gone through. What he had done once, he knew he could do again. His serenity astonished friend and foe alike.

In September of 1592, Saint John fell sick again. He suffered from fevers, and an infection in his foot refused to heal. Since there were no medical facilities in La Peñuela, John requested permission to go to a larger place. Friar Anthony of Jesus, who was now over eighty years of age, gave him the choice between Baeza and Ubeda, where the Carmelite monasteries were provided with some medical resources. In Baeza, where he had been Rector of the College, there were still many friends who remembered him. Some of the most powerful Carmelites there had been his disciples, and he could well expect gratitude and help. Precisely because he feared the softening effect of luxury, or at least of comfort, and of the care of devoted friends, friar John of the Cross chose to go to Ubeda to be among strangers.

The trip was difficult and long. Mounted on a small mule, John of the Cross suffered continuous pain. It was hard for him to stay on his mount because his leg was so inflamed and sensitive. He was hardly able to eat anything, and the fever blurred his sight and chilled his bones. The journey was slow, and when, at night fall, Saint John and his companion arrived in the town of Ubeda, the Prior Francisco Crisóstomo offered the father of his Reformed Order the poorest and smallest cell in his convent. There was only a bed and a crucifix in the room reserved for the ailing old friar.

### III  *Last Illness and Death*

John of the Cross had been deprived of all power and office. His cell was bare, and no entertainment, comfort, or consolation was at hand. He was again a humble friar—as humble and as poor as when he had started on the road to perfection in the hut at Duruelo. The only difference now was that he knew he did not have much time left. Although he had written from La Peñuela that his sickness was trivial and that he would recover in a short time, he must have known that his strength had been sapped. Even the unfriendly Prior noticed that something was seriously wrong and had a doctor called.

When Antonio de Villarreal, a physician in town, arrived the next morning, the five sores in John's foot had burst. Pus and blood were oozing. The doctor saw the need to open the ulcers and drain them. Without anesthetic, he proceeded to cut a deep incision, reaching the bone. The operation gave some relief but John of the Cross had to lie in bed. In the following days, he lay alone. The Prior visited him only to upbraid him and accuse him of a hundred imaginary crimes and imperfections. He ordered the brothers not to go near him. When charitable ladies in town offered their services to wash the sick man's linen and change the dressing of his wounds, the Prior refused his permission. He did not allow the townspeople to provide food for Saint John's sustenance.

The Prior of La Peñuela and many of the friars were grieved when they learned of the cruel treatment John was subjected to. They found ways to inform the Provincial, who was the very old and venerable Friar Antonio de Jesús, John's former prior in Duruelo. Antonio hastened to visit his old friend. When he saw the truth of the report, he censured the Prior of Ubeda and ordered some comfort of music and nourishment for John of the Cross. During the few days of his stay at Ubeda, Friar Antonio tried to cheer John, whom he visited often. After he left, since his example and his admonitions had succeeded in convincing the community that John deserved sympathy and love, the friars tried to console and help him, and even the Prior relented in his treatment of the dying friar.

It was, alas, too late. John himself begged that no music be played; he did not want to be distracted from the pain he thought was given to him for purification. As he lay in bed, his body began to be covered with sores. First, two large ulcers were found in the back, and were opened. Then a large sore developed between his shoulder blades. More sores covered his body, and the inflammation in his leg grew worse in spite of surgery.

In the first days of December, the physician made it clear to John that he could not hope to recover. He had only a few days to live. The last test was at hand. The remaining days he spent reading or listening to passages of religious books read to him. Occasionally he would listen to music or to the recitation of his own verses that promised the return of the rapture he had known in moments of meditation and fervor. He continued to reflect now on the futility of all things human and to long for the bliss he had named in enigmatic words during the suffering in his cell.

He knew now he would soon be delivered from the last imprisonment. On the night of the 14th of December of 1591, after having prepared his soul through confession and communion, he consoled with sweet conversation the young priests who had come to his side. Everybody was shaken, while John of the Cross was serene and happy. The distant murmur of matins could be heard when John ceased his exhortations for the last time. Those who had heard him knew he had just paused in his work. The words he had repeated so often were now to be repeated without the changes of his inflexion and reworking; they belonged to the world now. The thoughts and the rhythms he had left in manuscripts were copied by disciples who remembered him in the convents at Beas or Granada. His example lived on in the memory of those who had loved him. Many years later their manuscripts were to be printed, and the words he had uttered were to become all that was left of him.

John of the Cross had lived less than fifty years. Of the external experiences of success and power he had known little or nothing. Of poverty and suffering he had known as much as man can know. From childhood to adolescence, from youth to manhood and maturity, he had been schooled in pain and renunciation. He had had as many opportunities as any man in his time and place to grab security or worldly gain, but had spurned every chance. He had instead been steadfast and loyal to his one ambition to learn and to understand. He had been ill since adolescence and had suffered from unexplained fevers and excruciating pains. But his will had conquered pain and disease, poverty and calumny, temptation and power. What was left of him was only the light of a thought so clear that generation after generation would return to it again and again.

# CHAPTER 5

# The Doctrine of Saint John of the Cross

*Está ya medianamente declarado y dado a entender
(aunque harto menos de lo que ello es), cuántos sean
los bienes que consigo trae el alma, y cuán dichosa
ventura le sea al que por ella pasa.*
    *Noche oscura*, Libro II, Capítulo XXII

(I have shown and explained inadequately [but a
great deal less than the fact is], how many are the
blessings that the soul obtains, and what a delightful
happiness it is for the person who goes through it
[i.e., the dark night].
    *Dark Night*, Book II, Chapter XXII)

THE student from Medina del Campo, who had earned his
keep doing the most menial labors in a charity hospital,
had lived a full life and reached the end in peace and serenity.
He had done what he had set out to do. The accidental poverty
of a childhood without a father had evolved into the essential
poverty of renunciation. His desire for learning had transformed
itself into a zeal of faith. His daily service to the sick had expanded into service to every soul in need of the compassion of
his words. Yet, all that his life had accomplished died when he
did, except the pages into which he had poured the thoughts
that had come to him in his imprisonment and in the years of
quiet recollection in El Calvario or Granada. What he had taught
the young aspirants in convent and monastery, the words of
persuasion he had preached in the countryside had now been
left in manuscripts copied by devout nuns. All these pages spoke
endlessly of a way to the bliss he had known, and his followers
returned to his pages to be comforted in their suffering. Once
and again, his admirers copied poems and treatises, until some
of them were finally printed in 1618. Since then, both prose and
poetry have been read devoutly in the original Spanish and in the
many translations into French, English, German, Italian, and
other languages.

Since most of Saint John's poems were written before the treatises, and most of the latter are arranged as stanza by stanza commentaries on three of his poems, it is easily assumed that the poems are first in importance and were thought out before the prose. Saint John must have used the same ideas, though, in his teaching before writing the poems, and there is obviously a preparation both in doctrinal beliefs and technical skill that must have preceded the writing of poetry. The precedence of the doctrine in time is not just a conjecture. There is a passing reference by Saint Theresa to the youthful compositions of Saint John, who had written letters and was known as a persuasive and eloquent teacher. Furthermore, the poems themselves are based on solid doctrinal thought. But our immediate impression is not completely wrong: the experience of mystical knowledge has been transmitted through the poetry of Saint John, which is so intense that even maladroit translations convey some of its power. On the other hand, it is so carefully structured that only with an understanding of his doctrine can it be fully understood.

For the readers of Saint John in the sixteenth and seventeenth centuries the poems were only the testimony of an experience in which they were ultimately interested, while for us they are all of the experience. For them the attainment of this experience was a goal to be reached through the study of Saint John's prose. The poetry was only incidental. His contemporaries and those that followed them were directly preoccupied with his thought, his admonition, and his teachings. While the poetry tried to give expression to the unutterable bliss attained, the prose showed the way to its attainment, and they, unlike us today, paid more attention to the lesson than to the rapture.

All the writings of Saint John are concerned with the central problem of the union of the soul with God. His aim is to obtain an absolute knowledge of the universe transcending the knowledge of sensory perception or logical inference. His views are not, and could not have been, original in essence, since his mystical preoccupation was an experience shared through the centuries by many thinkers of the Western and Eastern worlds.

In most things Saint John follows the teaching of his predecessors. As most mystic writers, he sees the need of a long preparation, which leads the aspirant to the first delights of contemplation. There is in this first stage an assurance that the soul is no longer a captive of the concerns of the mundane world and its many material interests. The initiated is not free, however, of all pain or suffering. He can and must fall again and again into the doubt and the painful dryness of repeated purification. Independently of their merits or hard work, a few aspirants may attain through their endless efforts the highest accomplishment of union with the divine, together with the joys of illumination. Three stages, or ways, can then be discerned, and many mystic writers had already named them: purification or purgation, illumination or contemplation, and union. They are at the same time successive and simultaneous stages, since the last one cannot be attained without passing through the second, or the second one without passing through the first, but the experience of the three continue to exist in the last one and none of them is ever completely discarded in favor of the next one.

In Saint John there is no deviation from the age-old pattern. Mystical knowledge—the illumination of an inward certainty not supplied by the senses or by reason—is attained only after a previous surrender to a systematic deprivation of the pleasures and concerns that surround the life of this world. Before such illumination is attained, "there must be a period of severe probation, lasting often many years, and separating it from the previous state, which may have been one of most exalted virtue. Probably, many whom the Catholic Church honours as saints have never received this singular gift. But, in reading the biography of such as have been favoured with it, we shall invariably find that the possession of it has been preceded, not only by a trying course of dryness, weariness of spirit, insipidity of devotional duties, and, what is infinitely worse, dejection, despondency, temptation to give all up in disgust, and utmost despair."[1]

This period of severe probation is part of every theory of theological mysticism. In Saint John's writing there is a study of its significance that follows traditional belief in its detailed concern with the many possibilities of error and the meticulous description of all facets of the preparation. His doctrinal thought becomes original only in his view of the purification—which he called the Dark Night—and in the expression in poetic terms of the bliss of the completion of the experience.

As a writer Saint John belongs to his age. His treatises are heavily armored with biblical quotations and references. His thought is well balanced and always in submissive accord with the teachings of Saint Thomas Aquinas. But his experience bursts through his lines. Time and time again his writings acquire the forcefulness and vivid originality of a personal narrative. Although his prose rarely approaches the intensity of his poetry, there are some passages of great emotional power here and there which remind us that there is more than dry lesson and repetitious doctrine. In such passages and in his poetry, we feel the very intimate relation of Saint John to his personal God in an experience that was possible in the Spain of his day only because religion had been debated with an intense emotion and made actual by the squabbles and dissension of many opponents. In this sense, and perhaps even in a more direct way, Spanish mysticism owes its existence at least in part to the *illuminati* who stirred the religious conscience of Spaniards in the sixteenth century.

## I  *The Dark Night of the Soul*

From the *illuminati* comes the concern with personal experience that characterizes Spanish mystical writings of the sixteenth century. But against the *illuminati* were directed Saint John's powerful denunciations of all external demonstrations and visions that for him were not to be interpreted as supernatural. Saint John repeatedly cautioned the neophyte against the seduction of easy belief in hallucination produced by the desire to escape the rigor of study and penance. He insisted on the need of retracing the steps of tradition in obedience and humility. In this way, his writings had to repeat the lessons of his predecessors, and their originality and forcefulness depended on the presence of a vigorous personality remembering his own experience, not on the contortion of literary artifice.

The treatises of Saint John are written with the certainty that there is usefulness in the words offered to the reader. As a consequence, the prose may seem unduly harsh and didactically monotonous since it is the prose of a teacher who is sure of the undivided attention of his disciples. He neither courts them nor does he purposely avoid the seduction of elegance or the prolixity of detailed explanation. What his readers are seeking is the kernel of thought, but they do not fret at digressions. Into his discussion, Saint John weaves all possible recollection of the dogma or Church writings and, quite often, biblical quotations. He was imbued with the spirit of the Bible, knew it verse for verse, and could recite from almost any book or chapter by memory. Nevertheless, he never imitated or recalled parable or story for the sake of embellishing his thought or for the purpose of interpreting biblical passages. On the contrary, his use of the Bible is curiously original in that he tries to explain his experience and clarify his thought by means of the passages he recalls.[2]

Saint John used the material stored in his memory during his years as student and teacher to sustain the structure of his own reasoning. And, although at every turn of the page there may be a maxim or a quotation or a reminiscence, the total architecture is surprisingly original. The clarity of his views and the intensely personal tone of his sentences become more striking when we realize that the system within which he worked was a composite of a long tradition of belief and reflection.

Concept by concept, then, the whole architecture of thought in Saint John's explanation of the ways to union with the divine has its basis and its origins in the well-established foundations of faith. There is even a long tradition behind one of the most arresting concepts in his writings: the often repeated image of darkness. The "Dark Night of the Soul" is Saint John's name for the situation of the soul bent on being deprived of all joys and worldly attachments, but not yet filled with the bliss of discovery.

The origin of this mystical figure has been traced to the medieval English mystic Walter Hylton.[3] Scholars have found analogies with religious concepts in Arabic texts of the fifteenth century which were undoubtedly the sources for many Spanish writers, and have compared in detail Spanish mysticism to the texts of many religious writers of Northern Europe. Certainly no concept is ever entirely our own or ever entirely borrowed. What is important, however, is how the concept is appropriated by a new mind, interested primarily in expressing the totality of thought, not in finding adornment in fragments recollected from readings. Saint John is perhaps the first to see in this darkness, in this night of despair, the joys to come, an anticipation of another moment, and thus he praises darkness as part of divine light. Perhaps it is in Saint John's novelty that the meta-physical poet Henry Vaughn learned to see night in the divinity:

> There is in God—some say—
> A deep, but dazzling darkness.
> "The Night"

From this initial emotional discovery stems the power and originality of Saint John's reasoning. He directs his mind to the study of the preliminary experience of darkness as a prologue to the reaching out for divine union. In this way, his prose treatises become an introduction to the poems which they explain, and the crowning experience of poetry is possible only after the arduous learning of penance and suffering.

Saint John distinguishes different kinds of darkness in this night of the soul: the night of the senses and the night of the spirit, to which we may add the night of faith. In the night of Saint John there is absence of light and also deprivation of the comforts of sensory perception and knowledge—an intense lone-liness in which the soul seeks the extreme nakedness of its essence. The will to produce an absolute void in the soul proceeds to further deprivations through the sacrifice of intellect, the surrender of the power of reasoning, and, through surrender of the self, to the imaginary concept of the absolute or even of nothingness. This void is necessary for the reception of the divine Guest, and the aspiring soul has to strive to attain it through sacrifice.

For Saint John of the Cross, as we have seen, the Dark Night of the Soul is a long journey in which the first step is the night of the senses. In this darkness, the soul suffers and is deprived of all means of sensory knowledge. Next comes the Dark Night of Faith, which is dark because it refuses all rational knowledge, and the Dark Night of the Spirit, which is dark and painful because all manner of thought, even knowledge through intuition, prayer, or miraculous revelation, has to be sacrificed in order to achieve the absolute void necessary to discover the nature of the Divinity. Essentially, of course, this ascent is predicated on the belief that nothing that is known is to be confused with the supreme perfection of God. And, consequently, paying at-tention to anything at all would detract from thinking about God.

"This void which Saint John of the Cross demands as a prerequisite condition for mystical union with God is something special in the supernatural order,"[4] which can only be accomplished through the suffering of deprivation in darkness. But what makes Saint John's thought most original, we have seen before, is the presence of his experience in the midst of his reasoning, and this experience is seen in his attitude. For Saint John the suffering of these nights is a joy in itself because in recollecting the sorrow and the pain he sees only that it is necessary for the greatest bliss. His rapture is such that he insists on the praise of the night because it leads into the assurance of the greatest knowledge beyond understanding.

What surprises and seduces in Saint John is his glorying in the distress of the night and his desire for its darkness, which he considers a welcome necessity and consequently a preparatory joy. Perhaps this is the meaning a modern poet wants us to read in his prayer for a gift similar to the experience of Saint John. And his use of terms makes it clear that Rainer Maria Rilke was following closely in the footsteps of the saint:

> Take one, Lord, make him glorious, make him great,
> and grant a night, when mankind may receive
> that which no human depths has trodden yet,
> a night, where into bloom all things may break,
> make them more fragrant than the lilac, make
> their lull more soothing than your wind can give,
> make them more joyful than Jehoshaphat.[5]

Saint John had known this night, had suffered the emptiness of renunciation of all pleasure, all emotion, all attachment, and all thought. And he knew the end of his night: the light that comes out of darkness. He believed he knew how to teach others to attain it, hence his doctrinal treatises. He was also impelled by a force he did not understand to give poetic form to his emotion, hence his mystical poems. He thought both were linked as part of the same experience and doctrine, but we, as his readers, have separated them and we use them for different purposes and in different ways. It is quite possible that we are wrong. It is also probable that his thought is valid in different ways for different people, and that both he and posterity are

right or, at least, justified in their understanding of his experiences.

## II   *The Three Ways: Purification, Illumination, and Union*

The purification of the soul is the first step in the long road
to the rewards of ecstasy. At first, the obstacles that prevent the
attainment of perfection are the sinful occupations of the mind
and the lingering enjoyment of human relations, emotional attachment, and minor pleasures and comforts. The necessary
beginning must then be a constant self-denial and deprivation
of all possible material pleasure: a life of alert asceticism. This
is the stage of purification, in a sense a preliminary state, but
also a road to be traversed constantly and consistently both before
and after the attainment of perfection. In perfection there would
be no more need of striving, but perfection is momentary, and
attachment to the delights of a special kind of thought or
knowledge can become imperfection. Since every possible
thought is merely an approximation to the divine, there is no
way but the pursuit of a complete void, in which the soul must
know nothing and be nothing. In the last stage of perfection,
the soul must be free from everything no matter how spiritual
it may seem, since everything because it exists is a creature and
not the creator.

This first Way of Purification, the Purgative Way, leads to
peace, in the same way as the second, the Illuminative Way,
leads to truth, and the third, the Unitive Way, leads to love.
If these metaphors clearly referred to three successive stages,
it would be easy to explain and understand the process of
mystical inquiry. But, from the very beginning, even in the first
way of purification that seems clearly preliminary, the process
is a continuum in which the truth of contemplation as well as
the delight of union are prefigured in the joy of darkness, and,
at the same time, the ultimate union requires the constant
watchfulness of purification. The three ways overlap and "the
exercises prescribed are needed simultaneously at every stage of
the spiritual life. The first is concerned with the expulsion of sin,
the second with the imitation of Christ, and the third with the
'reception of the Bridegroom.' In the first two the soul is predominantly active, in the third predominantly passive, and . . .

in this last, meditation scarcely exists, having become unnecessary."[6]

In the process of asceticism, purification of the soul may
reach an inconceivable degree of minuteness. In a sense, even
attachment to certain forms of prayer may become an imperfection that must be conquered. The thought of God in itself is
too human to be acceptable as substitute for the experience of
the absolute. Only when illumination, that is to say, contemplation of the magnitude, infinity, and perfection of God, is possible,
has the soul entered the second stage, and is no longer a prey
to its own finite inferiority, although the first stage of purgation
has not been abandoned or forgotten.

The third stage in the process—the union in ecstasy—is absolutely different in its essence from the preceding two, although
it is obtained through the experience of purification and illumination and it contains them still. For Saint John this last stage,
or unitive way, means "the total transformation of the soul with
all its faculties from its unlikeness to likeness with God."[7] This
stage cannot be reached by the effort of the unguided soul.
Therefore the passage from purification and illumination to union
cannot be conceived of as an ascent or as progress toward
perfection because it is not reached by continuing efforts along
the same road, but rather, and only, through the willingness of
the divinity to give of itself to the soul.

The method of mystical knowledge, especially in the treatises
of Saint John, is one of rejection of all sensory delight, even the
sensory delights supplied by the inner vision of thought and
imagination. Continuous rejection and denial at every step of
achieved perfection must bring a desolate peace to the soul
which strives to attain the maximum detachment, to annihilate
all its powers in order to preserve only its own essence. Although
the soul by itself is incapable of the attainment which may or
may not be given to it, the efforts of purification and the knowledge of illumination do not cease even when the ecstasy of
union is reached. On the contrary, after ecstasy has been granted
there must continually be a preparation for the advent of the
union, and, when the union has been achieved, the preparation
must continue to assure the existence of the union: "There can
hardly be a question of the work being divided into three ways
or states of purification, illumination, and union. These are rather

three effects linked to one another throughout the whole life of grace and during the whole mystical way, even though one or the other is more emphasized at the different stages."[8]

In Saint John's view of the mystical experience, then, the purgative way is equated with the night of the senses, and the night of faith as the night of the spirit is related to the illuminative way. When both are completed, and while both are continuing, the unitive way may be reached. The full fruition of union is understood as the Spiritual Marriage—a form of knowledge through ecstasy that only a disorderly utterance of words can recall. The logic of reasoning, even the inner correlation of inference within what must be based on non-rational thought, is now impossible. Only the power of the poetic word can evoke in the mind a glimpse of the emotion remembered from such an experience. For this reason, the prose treatises of Saint John reach only the threshold of union, and are, in this sense, an introduction and basis for the poetry they explain.

### III   *Poetry and Doctrine*

Saint John of the Cross composed most of his poems, and the prose treatises explaining them, from 1578, when poetry burst forth in his life, to 1585, when the cares of office brought a slackening of his efforts as a writer. The three major poems, "Noche oscura del alma" ("Dark Night of the Soul"), "Cántico espiritual" ("Spiritual Canticle"), and "Llama de amor viva" ("Living Flame of Love") are explained in the three treatises of the same titles, of which the *Spiritual Canticle* is incomplete. *La subida del Monte Carmelo (Ascent of Mount Carmel)* is a fourth treatise which explains the poem "Dark Night of the Soul" and, in many ways, parallels the treatise on this poem. Undoubtedly, the best modern editions are inaccurate in some details, since no autographed copy of Saint John's writing exists. But on the whole, we may be satisfied that his thought has not been distorted. Modern emendations, based on comparison of several manuscripts, have made possible the reading of satisfactory texts of both poems and prose works.

In the prose explanations of his poetry, Saint John stops short when he has to face the examination of the last stage of the process: union or ecstasy. The poetry, on the other hand, always recalls the state of ecstasy which it cannot describe. The prose is, then, the intellectual preparation for the experience on which the poetry reflects. The experience itself is repeatedly said to be indescribable, in passages of both prose and verse in which exclamatory phrases succeed one another. The imagination must supply the missing moment of conceptual understanding.

If we consider the events in their literalness, it seems that the eight months in the prison of Toledo were for Saint John the road to ecstasy. After that, years of peace and reflection were spent explaining the value of the mystical revelation. But the facts are not that simple and clear. At least one poem, "Living Flame of Love," was written after his imprisonment, and probably the "Spiritual Canticle"—a central document—was completed some time after his escape.

At the same time, it is inconceivable that the architecture of thought and doctrine Saint John expounds in his treatises on his poems should not have existed in his mind before the imprisonment. If it had not existed, his teaching and, indeed, his intellectual life before 1578 would have been so utterly different from his life afterwards that his disciples and friends would have recognized a new man. But nobody was surprised by his thought, or even by the poetry he had brought out of prison. We must then accept the existence of a long preparation before writing and a long maturing of thought after the writing of Saint John's poetry.

And yet, the crucial moment, the experience of blinding light in his cell in Toledo, remains forever unexplained. It is this torturing vision of inconceivable happiness that became the center of speculation and recollection in the life of John of the Cross. When he was asked about his sojourn in prison, he himself was wont to say that he had received favors of such worth that a lifetime in prison could not repay for them. But he did not claim that the words he had written were ever dictated to him. He could only say that some lines had come to him at times, and, at other times, he had searched for other lines.

The study of the doctrine of Saint John of the Cross in his prose is of great help in the understanding of his poetry. The study of his poetry is of great help in the understanding of his prose treatises. The biographical details gathered by his followers after his death are also of help when we try to understand his poetry and his doctrine. But neither biography nor doctrine, neither verse nor anecdote can ever explain how he reached the state of union or describe the ecstasy his poems name again and again. Hallucination or naked thought, grace or human effort, intellectual endeavor or emotional outburst, the words are ours to repeat, and they recreate an unnamed experience, a journey, in which the mind is expanded beyond its usual meager range, and the absolute visits it to bring the reassurance of a peace and a knowledge never to be understood.

# CHAPTER 6

## The Revelation of Poetry

*Por la secreta escala disfrazada.*
*"Noche oscura del alma"*

(Disguised, by the secret staircase.
"Dark Night of the Soul")

POETRY and music, as well as sculpture and painting, played a role in the everyday life of Saint John. Other friars and nuns praised his drawings and carvings. We know he liked to sing, and an anecdote even refers to his enthusiastic dancing on one occasion. All these artistic activities, however, were only a part of his religious vocation. He drew a view of Mount Carmel in which he tried to synthesize the teachings of his mystical doctrines. He carved a wooden Christ. His singing and his poetry were always an expression of his faith. He knew little and cared not at all for the study of technique or theory, although his skilful versification proves that he must have received some training. Only once did Saint John comment on a technical point in the writing of verse. In the introduction to the treatise on the *Living Flame of Love,* Saint John refers the reader to the works of the early sixteenth-century poet Juan Boscán. He quotes a few lines of Garcilaso de la Vega, whose works were published together with those of Boscán, to indicate that he is using the same stanza pattern of six lines previously used by Garcilaso in a poem Saint John believed to be by Boscán.[1] It is obvious from this commentary that Saint John was not ignorant, as he hardly could be, of the conventions of Renaissance poetry.

Saint John, as most Spanish poets of his time, used verse forms that were known in the language before the assimilation of Italianate patterns, as well as the new stanzas and lines that were being evolved by Spanish poets. Some verses in the works of Saint John are akin to the old accentual systems of versification kept in popular songs and known in Spain for many centuries:

*Qué bien sé yo la fonte que mana y corre,*
*Aunque es de noche.*
> *Cantar del alma que se huelga*
> *de conoscer a Dios por fe.*

(Well I know the fountain that runs and flows
Although it's night.
> Song of the soul that is glad
> to know God by faith.)

After these lines the poem continues with couplets of long
lines interrupted by the refrain, *aunque es de noche,* in a pattern
that harkens back to medieval songs of love. The lines themselves, the use of a refrain, the repetition of a concept throughout
the poem, and the arrangement are traditional in Spanish. Saint
John used also the traditional form of the *romance* (ballad
meter), a long poem composed of eight-syllable lines with a
vowel rhyme or assonance at the end of every other line; he
even used this form for a translation, or rather paraphrasing,
of the Psalm "Super flumina Babylonia." Some of his minor
poems take a well-known line or couplet and add to it several
stanzas or *glosas* (glosses) of commentary, each one ending with a
repetition of the traditional verses. This procedure was a literary
fashion of the time, and in Saint John it may seem somewhat
artificial in comparison to his best poems.

> *Vivo sin vivir en mí,*
> *Y de tal manera espero,*
> *Que muero porque no muero.*
>
> *Esta vida que yo vivo*
> *Es privación de vivir;*
> *Y así, es contino morir*
> *Hasta que viva contigo;*
> *Oye, mi Dios, lo que digo,*
> *Que esta vida no la quiero;*
> *Que muero porque no muero.*
>
> (I live, but yet do not live
> In me. My hopes fly so high that
> I die because I do not die.
>
> The life I lead is only
> A way of not living, that is,
> It will be a constant death

Until I live in you.
Listen, my God, to what I say:
This life I do not want, for
I die because I do not die.)

The opening stanza had been known in Spanish for at least a century for it was part of a poem published in fifteenth-century songbooks and probably sung as a love poem. Both Saint John and Saint Theresa appropriated these verses and made them the expression of their longing for the bliss of heaven. They both wrote on, adding to the lines explanatory stanzas as was the custom in the literature of their age.

Many songs and poems of popular origin found their way to Saint John's thoughts and were paraphrased and turned into expressions of his religious hopes and desires. For instance, a popular ditty was the source in which he learned a peculiarity of technique he used at least twice: the repetition of a syllable.

> *Por toda la hermosura*
> *Nunca yo me perderé,*
> *Sino por un no sé* qué
> *Que se alcanza por ventura.*
>
> (I will never lose my soul
> For all the beauty the world holds,
> Only for one thing that I do not know
> And that is only found by luck.)

In this example the repetition of a monosyllable makes the mind pause and wonder about the mysterious thing it cannot name. There is in this artifice a preparation of a line of the "Cántico espiritual." Unfortunately we do not have enough information about the dates of composition of these poems. We cannot say then that the poet attempted here imperfectly what he would do with consummate mastery later. Nor can we say that he is here trying to repeat a sucessful line of his own. On the other hand, there is no doubt that he knew the popular poetry of his age before writing either this short poem or the "Spiritual Canticle" and, therefore, we are able to state that he inherited themes and technical devices from a rich tradition which he in his turn enriched with his artistry and his depth.

Translation is a valid exercise in literary apprenticeship, as is the imitation of others and the use of these *glosas*. Even the varied meters used by the poet indicate a desire to experiment and a conscious attempt to improve. The unusual in Saint John is not the absence of hesitation, but rather the accomplishment in his apprenticeship. He did not go through long periods of change to polish his expression and clarify his thought. The few poems he has left us are all mature. Among them, the three he chose to comment on are the most important and complete, but the others, with a few exceptions, are still read and enjoyed and are very much a part of the Spanish tradition.

The patterns of line and stanza adapted to Spanish from the Italian by Boscán and Garcilaso and used by all religious poets of the sixteenth century had been introduced earlier, when the influence of Dante and Petrarch spread over Europe in the fifteenth century. Although quite often their rhythmic habits in Spanish led poets astray, the heroic verse of Italian poetry was finally turned into an eleven-syllable line, with accents on the sixth syllable or on the fourth and eighth besides the necessary final accent. This line was slowly accepted for poetic composition. It could be used in certain arrangements of rhyme such as that of the sonnet or the *terza rima*, both adaptations from the Italian. It could also be used in combinations with shorter lines of seven syllables. In the fifteenth century, the *Sonetos fechos al itálico modo* (*Sonnets in the Italian Manner*) of the Marquis of Santillana were the most successful attempts at assimilation of the new forms.

In the early sixteenth century there were numerous attempts at adaptations of the Italianate forms. Juan Boscán, already mentioned, was a gentleman of the court of Charles V; prompted by the Italian ambassador, Andrea Navagero, he tried his hand at the new forms. His friend, the courtier and captain of the army of Charles V, Garcilaso de la Vega, also tried, Garcilaso knew Latin and Italian well, and, in his poems, he weaves together the themes of Classical antiquity, the forms of the new Italian poetry, and the depth of his feelings and thought. When he died at the age of thirty-three, in the assault on the tower of Muy in 1536, he left a tiny collection of poetry that was published by the widow of Juan Boscán with the title of *Las obras de Boscán y algunas de Garcilaso de la Vega repartidas en quatro libros* in 1543.

What in the sixteenth century seemed the joint effort of two talented friends has been changed by history. Boscán is remembered today mostly as a friend of Garcilaso, while Garcilaso is considered among the greatest poets of the language. His poems deal mostly with themes of unrequited love or of sorrow upon the death of the beloved—themes hardly suitable for religious meditation. He was the master of the hyperbaton; he could establish a new sequence of words in which the logic of grammatical order was subordinated to the necessity of expression and in which each word he used acquired the full emotional impact he wanted. The spell of Garcilaso's words and the cadence of his lines found their way to influence even those writers who were concerned with religious goals and did not approve of his themes. Very soon after his death, his poems were rewritten with subtle changes that transformed their meaning without losing completely the charm of a word order that was then and still is of unequaled perfection in the Spanish language. In 1577 Sebastián de Córdoba rewrote Garcilaso's poems in *Las obras de Boscán y Garcilaso a lo divino* to give them religious significance. For instance, the beginning of the "First Eclogue,"

> *El dulce lamentar de dos pastores,*
> *Salicio juntamente y Nemoroso,*
> *he de contar*

> (The sweet lamentations of two shepherds,
> Salicio together with Nemoroso,
> I will relate)

became with Córdoba:

> *El dulce lamentar de dos pastores,*
> *Cristo y el pecador triste y lloroso,*
> *he de cantar.*

> (The sweet lamentations of two shepherds,
> Christ and the sad and tearful sinner
> I shall sing of.)

Among the metrical forms that Garcilaso's example made popular in Spanish was a combination of lines of seven and eleven syllables, known today as the *lira,* in which the first, third, and fourth lines of a five-line stanza are short, while the second and fifth are long. These lines have full rhymes that link first and third lines—both short—and the long second line with the fourth and fifth:

> *Si de mi baja lira*
> *Tanto pudiese el són, que en un momento*
> *Aplacase la ira*
> *Del animoso viento,*
> *Y la furia del mar y el movimiento . . .*
> > Garcilaso, "A la Flor del Gnido"

> (If of my humble lyre
> The sound could so prevail as in one moment
> To calm the anger
> Of the furious winds,
> And the choler of the sea and its tossing . . .
> > Garcilaso, to "The Flower of Gnido")

This stanzaic form became popular in many poems in which the religious sensibility of the age tried to express with the subtle vigor of Garcilaso very different emotions. Saint John used it for his major poems, except for a six-line variation in the "Living Flame of Love," a variation which he also appropriated from the works of Garcilaso, as acknowledged in his comment. The very ingenuousness of his remark proves that Saint John set little store by his knowledge of poetry or poetic technique, although it also seems to prove that he remembered passages of poetry easily. His extraordinary skill must then have been derived from his rich imitative memory rather than from assiduous study of the technical expertness of others.

Thus the linguistic and technical components of Saint John's poetry were those that were close to hand. A detailed analysis of his lines reveals many reminiscences of passages from the works of Garcilaso and others. At times, words of popular songs are repeated and, frequently, his imagery is derived from the Bible, especially from the "Song of Songs." Nonetheless, in his best poems, the elements he fused together are so completely transformed that the reader never feels the presence of an incongruous association even, for instance, when the Classical term "nymph" is used to refer to the maids of Judea.

Many writers attempted in the sixteenth century to write religious poetry in the forms of the newly acquired Italianate fashion or in the patterns of popular songs. There was a wealth of imitative poetry *a lo divino* which consisted in turning the poems of secular love into religious verse merely by means of a few changes of key words. But Saint John's extraordinary skill and faultless ear as well as the forceful originality of his thought set him apart from the many religious writers of his age.

Through the centuries his poetry has been imitated in a way that would have embarrassed him in his own day. The trappings of his meter and rhyme are repeated by many who would like to believe that their religious emotions need the expression of verse. Occasionally, the intimate simplicity of his appeal has been echoed with extraordinary success by Spanish poets of our own century who have learned from him the command of language needed for the expression of their own distinct emotions and doctrines. Juan Ramón Jiménez, one of the greatest of Spanish poets of the twentieth century, has applied the words of ecstasy to the rendering of the joy of intellectual discovery. In his poetry the experience of mystic union has become the rapture of understanding; his lyrical tone owes a great deal to the example of Saint John perpetuated in the language by many writers, Jiménez—who won the Nobel Prize in 1956—has held a position of leadership in the poetry of the Spanish language since the beginning of the century. His influence is comparable to that of Rainer Maria Rilke in German or W. B. Yeats or T. S. Eliot in English. All these twentieth-century poets have turned to the dark night of Saint John to find inspiration and strength in their search for purity of expression. In them Saint John's thought is given new life, although they search for a different peace in a world beset by different problems.

Of the few poems Saint John wrote, the readers and critics have selected consciously or unconsciously even fewer for their continued reading. When he first selected three of his poems for analysis and explanation, Saint John himself did not mean to perform any critical choice, but posterity has agreed with him and has set these three poems apart as those of greatest value because of the exquisite perfection of their form and because they deal most directly with the experience of ecstasy. A handful of poems besides these three are still of great value to us today, although in a different way and for different reasons, but others have been rejected as literature even though they may still be read for religious reasons.

As we have seen, the lines believed to have been the first Saint John composed while in prison form a short poem built around the refrain *Aunque es de noche* ("Although it's night"), in which eleven three-line stanzas develop the theme of certainty in knowledge and faith.

> *Aquella eterna fonte está ascondida,*
> *Que bien sé yo do tiene su manida,*
> *Aunque es de noche.*
> *Su origen no lo sé, pues no le tiene,*
> *Mas sé que todo origen de ella viene,*
> *Aunque es de noche.*
> *Sé que no puede ser cosa tan bella,*
> *Y que cielos y tierra beben de ella,*
> *Aunque es de noche.*

> (That eternal fountain is well hidden,
> And well I know where its source is,
> Although it's night.
> I do not know its origin, for it has none,
> But I do know that everything in it has its beginning,
> Although it's night.
> I know there cannot be a thing of such beauty,
> And that heavens and earth drink there,
> Although it's night.)

Repetition here, as in other instances in his poetry, adds to the emotional impact of the simple chain of reasoning. In another poem based on popular song themes, and expressed in octosyllabic lines in a stanzaic form we now know as the *redondilla*, the haunting call of mysterious forces is embodied in a huntsman's metaphor:

> *Tras de un amoroso lance*
> *Y no de esperanza falto,*
> *Volé tan alto, tan alto,*
> *Que le di a la caza alcance.*

> (In the quest of love
> —Not without hope, of course—
> I soared so high, so high,
> That I was able to catch my prey.)

Of all those poems which, compared with Saint John's major works, seem only the diversions of a great mind, readers have chosen the five quatrains of a bucolic love poem for their special affection. *Un pastorcico solo está penando* ("A shepherd is grieving in solitude") is the first line of this strange love pastoral. The shepherd's laments harken back to a bucolic tradition that Italy and Spain had inherited from ancient Greece. But the shepherd's love for a forgetful maiden is suddenly revealed as an experience of Christianity when the shepherd dies crucified on a tree:

> *Y al cabo de un gran rato se ha encumbrado*
> *Sobre un árbol; abrió sus brazos bellos,*
> *Y muerto se ha quedado, asido de ellos,*
> *El pecho del amor muy lastimado.*
>
> (And after a long while he climbed
> A tree and opened his wide arms,
> And dead he remains there, bound by his arms,
> His breast of love sorely wounded.)

Many of the traditional themes of pagan antiquity and of medieval love are fused in Saint John's thought and expression because in his century a new Humanism had invaded Europe with the cult of Greek and Roman letters, and his country accepted and worshipped novelties without ever forgetting the wealth of its own immediate past. Even though form and imagery could often come from literary sources, Saint John always managed to put a touch of imaginative sincerity in whatever he wrote. As we have seen, a restatement of a traditional paradox, *que muero porque no muero* ("I die because I do not die"), is the basis of one of his minor poems, but even this minor *glosa* has become a well-known and admired piece. Yet the extraordinary vividness of his three most important poems surpasses in artistry and emotion anything he or any other poet of his time wrote. In a language rich in religious writings, Saint John remains unique as the finest poet of mystic rapture with the *liras* of the "Dark Night of the Soul," the "Spiritual Canticle," and the "Living Flame of Love."

## I  *"Dark Night of the Soul"*

At the start of every spiritual quest there is a need to sacrifice what we have. The first step requires that we leave behind that which has been our concern and selfishness before we undertake the pursuit of something beyond. The soul speaks then of an attainment that is prefigured in the darkness of purification:

> En una noche oscura,
> Con ansias en amores inflamada,
> ¡Oh dichosa ventura!
> Salí sin ser notada,
> Estando ya mi casa sosegada.

> (In the darkness of the night,
> With love and longing seized,
> Oh delightful happiness!
> I went abroad unnoticed,
> All then being quiet in my house.)

Saint John's commentary on his poems, the treatises that explain his doctrine, make clear the allegorical meaning of each detail in this pursuit of the experience of ecstasy. The boldness of the attempt makes the two first lines of the stanza seem breathless in their sustained rhythm, broken by the exclamation of the third line and ending with the quiet music of the last verse in which the alliteration of the repeated "s" slows the pace and restores symmetry and peace to the world.

Only when all other desires are appeased is it possible to kindle the flame of a love greater and more pure than anything we have known. The soul can soar only when the senses and the faculties that house our pilgrim spirit have been silenced. In the symbolic correspondence of words and experience, the happiness of renunciation at the beginning of knowledge is rendered in a story of escape. The second stanza is apparently a repetition of the concepts, even the words, of the first one, but the concept of secrecy is here made more prominent as though its incidental appearance in the previous stanza had forced the mind to dwell on it and find the voluptuous pleasure of secrecy:

> A escuras, y segura,
> Por la secreta escala disfrazada,
> ¡Oh dichosa ventura!
> A escuras, y en celada,
> Estando ya mi casa sosegada.

> (In safety, in the dark,
> Disguised, by the secret staircase,

Oh delightful happiness!
In the dark, stealthily,
All then being quiet in my house.)

Because in its darkness the night itself is an intimation of the light to come, and because the renunciation is a prelude to acquisition, the poet can speak of a "fortunate night": *En la noche dichosa* (In the happiness of the night). The adjective "fortunate" (*dichosa*) appears for the third time in the third stanza of the poem, having been announced by the repetitious exclamation: *Oh dichosa ventura!* (Oh delightful happiness!) which occurs in both the first and second stanzas. The apparently unnecessary adjective here gives greater force to the tautological exclamation and seems to raise the value of this happiness beyond the power of words precisely because the adjective adds nothing to the meaning of the noun itself.

A rapture of liberation fills the first three stanzas of the "Dark Night of the Soul." Next, an inward turn towards the light "at the turning of the stairs" guides the protagonist in the certainty of his desire. The inner light, the light of faith, is kindled in this dark night of renunciation, when the soul has schooled itself in the difficult task of not fixing its attention on anything human or natural and has surrendered the powers of emotion and intellect. In the secret life of this renunciation nobody is witness to the new freedom, when the soul is freed from any desire of earthly things. Expressed in the metaphorical terms of a meeting of lovers, the soul hurries in the night to meet the one who is waiting:

> *En la noche dichosa,*
> *En secreto, que nadie me veía,*
> *Ni yo miraba cosa,*
> *Sin otra luz y guía*
> *Sino la que en el corazón ardía.*
> *Aquésta me guiaba*
> *Más cierto que la luz del mediodía,*
> *A donde me esperaba*
> *Quien yo bien me sabía,*
> *En parte donde nadie parecía.*

> (In the happiness of the night,
> Secretly, unseen by anybody,

Looking at nothing else,
With no other light or guide
Save that which was burning in my heart.
　This light guided me
More certain than the light of midday,
To where one awaited me
Whom I knew well
In a place where no one would appear.)

The light and the night become one, or, even better, have always been one, because they have been instrumental in bringing about the desired experience. Then night or darkness and deprivation are as dear as the light of reasoning and faith:

> ¡*Oh noche, que guiaste,*
> *Oh noche amable más que el alborada!*
> ¡*Oh noche, que juntaste*
> *Amado con amada,*
> *Amada en el Amado transformada!*

> (Oh night that was my guide,
> Oh night dearer than the dawn!
> Oh night, that joined
> Lover to beloved,
> Transforming the bride into the Lover!)

The experience of the Saint has been embodied in eight stanzas that transform a patient ascent into a headlong rush. All the steps of the poet's experience were necessary to produce the clear lines of these stanzas: his adolescent renunciation, his calm and determined study and reasoning; his ascetic withdrawal from all pleasures; and his suffering and his imprisonment. The reading of these forty lines can bring to the eager mind of today the same thrill of discovery, because poetry is born of the writer's experience and reproduces this experience in the reader. It is not necessary, however, that the experience of the reader should reproduce completely the experience of the author. The reader only summarizes in his mind the lives of the men who have lived before him. And today he is able to possess all of Saint John's experience of mystery in the reading of just a few of his words.

After passing from the rapture of sacrifice to the dawn of discovery, the journey is suddenly crowned with the fruition of love consummated. But this happiness is seen as recollection because the moment of attainment can be described only in the mirror of the past and in terms of human words of passion which serve only as intermediary signs for the understanding of the ultimate union. In the poems of Saint John, as traditionally in mystic writers, the union is viewed as the spiritual marriage of the soul or Bride and the divinity or Bridegroom.

> *En mi pecho florido,*
> *Que entero para él sólo se guardaba,*
> *Allí quedó dormido,*
> *Y yo le regalaba,*
> *Y el ventalle de cedros aire daba.*

> (On my flowering breast,
> That was saved only for him,
> There he fell asleep,
> And I caressed him,
> And a fan of cedar trees waved the air.)

Although the words are those of human passion, the surprising image of a huge fan of cedar trees teases the imagination and leads to regions far away, to regions seen only with an inward eye that is finally closed in the restful moment of an absolute sharing with the divinity when the self or soul is lost:

> *Quedéme, y olvidéme,*
> *El rostro recliné sobre el Amado,*
> *Cesó todo, y dejéme,*
> *Dejando mi cuidado*
> *Entre las azucenas olvidado.*

> (I stayed, lost to myself,
> My face upon my lover I laid,
> All endeavor ceased, I forgot myself,
> And all my cares were left
> Forgotten among the lilies.)

In this poetry the images of sensuous pleasure reproduce a spiritual joy. Saint John's commentary, if we go in search of accurate meaning, can turn a tower or the hair into symbols of theological virtues. But the reader of his poems feels rather the shudder of an exquisite pleasure when the senses are suspended.

*Con su mano serena*
*En mi cuello hería,*
*Y todos mis sentidos suspendía.*

(With its serene hand
My neck wounded,
And suspended every one of my senses.)

And yet the extraordinary depth of feeling, the strange words, and strange concepts make it impossible to read only on the level of sensuous experience. Attention requires a hidden meaning, and the words burst upon us and transport us in spite of the literalness of our minds.

The experience of mystic union of the soul and the creator has now been completed, the soul has found the divinity and can rest without apprehension or fear. It is only the recollection of this moment, though, that is captured in the words of the poem. The narration has brought us from the starting point of stepping forth stealthily into the darkness of the night to the ultimate in happy forgetfulness. The way of purification, in which the spirit strives to be free from the imperfections of everyday life, leads to the success of contemplation and union in steps of deliberate progress. But poetry flies over all the intermediate steps of hope and despair and gives us a synthesis which is placed by tradition at the beginning of a study of Saint John's thought, as we have seen, although it is impossible to ascertain the exact chronology of his writings. The "Dark Night of the Soul" is like the portal of a building. As an intimation of future knowledge, it summarizes all that is to be found; the "Spiritual Canticle" will immediately explore it in careful detail. Both poems are complete in themselves; both are utterances of a soul that has completed the cycle of discovery and returned to tell of the joy attained in a trip to the depths of oneself. Both poems also complement each other by expanding in one or synthesizing in the other case the same story of sacrifice, quest, and discovery. The poet felt he had to add a third account of blissful recollection, the "Living Flame of Love." Even this third poem, though, needs to be considered as a complete unit, not merely as a part of a larger whole. We have really three distinct views, not three stages of one view.

## II  "Spiritual Canticle"

Because the experience of which Saint John was writing is always the same, his poems as well as his prose may seem to repeat the same concepts. At times the phrasing itself may be familiar to the reader, who often hears echoes of John's poetry in the prose. This reiteration is necessary, no matter how rich the imagination of the poet, because the goal is not literary beauty for its own sake but an expression of the attainment of spiritual perfection. The repetition itself can be made into a technical resource, as with the insistence of the refrain or by dwelling on the same word as we have seen happen in the first stanzas of the "Dark Night of the Soul." It is also possible to repeat the same concept with different words to give expression to the sorrowful request of an impassioned love: *Decidle que adolezco, peno y muero.* (Tell him that I suffer, grieve, and die.)

When Saint John wrote his poems, the complicated conventions of our punctuation were not taught in schools or used with any regularity. He himself paid no attention to any division or pause except those of stanza, meter, line, and rhyme. For this reason, our reading in a modern version that has been skilfully rearranged, and in which relationships between the parts are established by commas, colons, and periods, may do violence to the poet's view of the flow of words. Unfortunately we cannot recapture his own reading, in which there must have been pauses, inflexions, and intonations which are forever lost, but which are intrinsically part of the meaning of his verse. Our punctuation is an attempt to restore the fullness of such meaning. At times, as for instance, when the line, *Decidle que adolezco, peno y muero,* is repeated today, the pause that precedes each repetition of the concept of suffering in three different words is quite probably close enough to the original reading. But the problem is quite different in the lines in which the soul apostrophizes the divine presence when this suddenly appears in the thirteenth stanza:[2]

> *Mi Amado, las montañas,*
> *Los valles solitarios nemorosos,*
> *Las ínsulas extrañas,*
> *Los ríos sonorosos,*
> *El silbo de los aires amorosos.*

> *La noche sosegada*
> *En par de los levantes de la aurora,*
> *La música callada,*
> *La soledad sonora,*
> *La cena, que recrea y enamora.*

(My Love, the mountain range,
The solitary melancholy valleys,
The islands far and strange,
The pleasant sounding rivers,
The whistling of loving breezes.
  The quiet night
Just before the coming of dawn,
The silent music,
The musical solitude,
The supper that entertains and enamours.)

There is no way to render in the modern version this exaltation of what seems to be disorder. As a catalogue, with commas, colons, and periods or any other intrusions, the chaotic flow intended becomes artificially trimmed. Originally the reading of these lines must have had a vigor we cannot recreate. Precisely because here the language does violence to logic, we suddenly become aware of an experience of emotion quite beyond the capacity of our minds to order it. But this experience is not chaotic or disorderly. It is an experience that embraces many objects and brings them together without need of a thread of logical connection. Mountains, valleys, remote islands, rivers, and breezes join night, music, and solitude. Had the author thought of a possible end to this sentence and then left it unfinished when the imperious force of the next stanza caught him? Did he intend to write a verbless sentence? These questions seem immaterial if we realize that the experience of readers through the centuries has been precisely that of putting together this disorderly enumeration without the use of logic.

The "Spiritual Canticle" is made up of dialogues in which universal forces or essences—the Soul, the Creator, the Creatures —act out the drama of the mystic experience. From the very first words, this poem, unlike the "Dark Night of the Soul," establishes the immediacy of the experience through the present tense. Instead of the narration of an unforgettable moment, this poem reproduces step by step the course of a search for the unknowable finally rewarded. The initial moment is the Bride's question of despair:

#### ESPOSA

*¿A dónde te escondiste,*
*Amado, y me dejaste con gemido?*
*Como el ciervo huiste,*
*Habiéndome herido;*
*Salí tras ti clamando, y eras ido.*

*    Pastores los que fuerdes*
*Allá por las majadas al otero,*
*Si por ventura vierdes*
*Aquel que yo más quiero,*
*Decidle que adolezco, peno y muero.*

*    Buscando mis amores,*
*Iré por esos montes y riberas,*
*Ni cogeré las flores,*
*Ni temeré las fieras,*
*Y pasaré los fuertes y fronteras.*

#### (BRIDE

Where are you hiding,
Beloved, having left me to moan?
Like the stag you fled
After wounding me;
I followed crying aloud, but you had gone.
    Shepherds, you that go
Through the sheepfolds to the hills,
If by chance you see
Him that I love most,
Tell him that I suffer, grieve, and die.
    Searching for my love
I will wander amongst mountains and rivers,
I will not gather flowers
Nor fear the prowling beasts,
And I will pass through all the forts and frontiers.)

Within the convention of the pastoral, and with recollections of the "Song of Songs," the wounded Bride goes out in search of the cause of her misery. She asks all living beings where to find her Creator and goes forth through all the dangers of natural reasoning. This is, of course, the first step to mystical knowledge: the discovery that it is through the beauty of the universe that we can discern the necessary cause of being. The presence of the divinity is felt in the reflection left in the creatures:

### RESPUESTA DE LAS CRIATURAS
*Mil gracias derramando,*
*Pasó por estos sotos con presura,*
*Y, yéndolos mirando,*
*Con sola su figura*
*Vestidos los dejó de hermosura.*

(ANSWER OF THE CREATURES
Showering a thousand graces,
In haste he passed through these groves,
And, as he looked on them,
By the mere sight of his face
He clothed them in beauty.)

The usual answers do not satisfy the Bride who requires the understanding of the ultimate cause, not just the view of the effects as shown by messengers: *Acaba de entregarte ya de vero* (Make the last surrender in full truth.) The answer of the creatures is never sufficient. Their words hide unutterable sounds which can be faintly heard when they speak. In order to render the unknowable comprehensible, a line of the poem dwells on the repetition of a syllable that seems to stutter in its impotence to name a mystery, making the reader pause to search for it: *Un no sé* qué que que*dan balbuciendo* (Of that something they leave half said.)

The first part of the poem deals then with the desire of the Bride for the accomplishment of that which has been promised in the natural order of things. In the convention of religion and mystic thought the union of the soul and the divinity has always been interpreted as a spiritual marriage, and, since the genders of the Spanish language favor it, the soul has become feminine and is known as the Bride. The masculine Creator is then referred to as the Bridegroom. This convention has seemed clumsy to some philosophical minds that object to the apparent confusion of realms between concepts and beings. But the language knows no closer relationship of emotion than passion, and thus it becomes poetically right to render the unthinkable and unknowable through the very words and forms that express the joys we do know. The climactic moment in the lamentations of the Bride is conveyed through a startling paradox in which the Creator is accused of not stealing the stolen heart of the bride:

*¿Por qué, pues has llagado*
*A aqueste corazón, no le sanaste?*
*Y pues me le has robado,*
*¿Por qué así le dejaste,*
*Y no tomas el robo que robaste?*

(Why, since you pierced
This heart, have you not healed it?
And since you have stolen it,
Why do you leave it
And do not take the plunder of your theft?)

The cognate accusative *robo,* in which the noun repeats the meaning of the verb *robar,* gives a strange forcefulness to the words of the Bride who has reached a state of utmost despair in her attempt to attain the promised reward of impossible satisfaction. She takes wing in this moment of excruciating pain and then hears the soothing words of the Bridegroom:

*ESPOSA*
*Apártalos, Amado,*
*Que voy de vuelo.*

*ESPOSO*
*Vuélvete, paloma,*
*Que el ciervo vulnerado*
*Por el otero asoma,*
*Al aire de tu vuelo, y fresco toma.*

(BRIDE
Look away, my Love,
For I am on the wing.

BRIDEGROOM
Turn back, dove,
The wounded hart
On the hill appears,
Refreshed by the wind of your flight.)

From here on, the dialogue is an exchange of vows and an apparently disordered presentation of the experience of total compenetration with the cosmos. A description of the Bridegroom in the present tense flows into a recollection of past favors which return to an affirmation of the total surrender of the soul:

> *Mi alma se ha empleado,*
> *Y todo mi caudal en su servicio:*
> *Ya no guardo ganado,*
> *Ni ya tengo otro oficio;*
> *Que ya sólo en amar es mi ejercicio.*

> (My soul is in his service
> And all my riches too,
> Flocks I no longer keep
> Nor any other work I have,
> My only duty now is to love.)

This certainty of the happiness of loving, not yet of being loved, is summarized paradoxically in the forceful last line of a stanza in which the impossible has become real:

> *Pues ya si en el ejido,*
> *De hoy más no fuere vista ni hallada,*
> *Diréis que me he perdido,*
> *Que andando enamorada,*
> *Me hice perdidiza, y fui ganada.*

> (So now, if in the common lands
> I am no longer found or seen,
> Say that I went astray,
> That being in love,
> I was lost, and I was found again.)

The last stanzas of the poem are a dramatic interplay in which the union of love is fulfilled in anticipation and retrospection at the same time:

> *Detente, cierzo muerto;*
> *Ven, Austro, que recuerdas los amores,*
> *Aspira por mi huerto,*
> *Y corran tus olores,*
> *Y pacerá el Amado entre las flores.*

> (Cease, Northern gale;
> Come, Southern breeze, recalling love,
> Breathe in my orchard,
> Pervaded by sweet scents,
> And the Beloved will tarry among the flowers.)

The exchange of love, request, and granting reaches its culmination when the Bridegroom defines the solitude of the Soul in love and confesses to his own solitude and need for love:

> *En soledad vivía,*
> *Y en soledad ha puesto ya su nido,*
> *Y en soledad la guía*
> *A solas su querido,*
> *También en soledad de amor herido.*

> (In solitude she lived,
> And in solitude she has built her nest,
> In solitude she is guided
> By her solitary lover,
> Also in solitude wounded by love.)

In this last stanza, the word *soledad* is repeated four times and reinforced by the adverb *a solas*. The predominance of noun over verb and adjective[3]—even adjectival and verbal meanings are conveyed by nouns—makes for a concentration of meaning that reaches the very limit of the possibilities of language. In the last verse the ambiguity of never deciding whether the Bridegroom has been wounded by love in his solitude or wounded in the solitude of his love, conjures the immense conflict of an imagination that can believe that the divinity itself harbors love for the human soul and is as much in need of their union as is the mind of man.

The last five stanzas try to depict the bliss known and expected in terms of comparisons which bring to the mind the exquisiteness of the paradoxical joy and suffering of mystic knowledge:

> *Y luego a las subidas*
> *Cavernas de la piedra nos iremos,*
> *Que están bien escondidas,*
> *Y allí nos entraremos,*
> *Y el mosto de granadas gustaremos.*

> (And then to the very high
> And rocky caverns we will go,
> Which are well hidden,
> And there we will enter,
> And we will taste of the wine of pomegranates.)

### III  *"Living Flame of Love"*

Towards the end of the "Spiritual Canticle," the Bride exhorts her beloved and speaks about the repetition of the happiness already known. The poem completes the narrative by asserting the continuing value of the experience of union, which cannot be exhausted, and describing in another catalogue of disorder the effects and causes of delight:

> *El aspirar del aire,*
> *El canto de la dulce Filomena,*
> *El soto y su donaire,*
> *En la noche serena*
> *Con llama que consume y no da pena.*

> (The softness of the air,
> The sweet song of Philomel,
> The charm of the grove,
> In the quiet of the night
> With fire that consumes without hurting.)

The transformation of the soul into spirit, its return to the original force that gave it being is defined through the paradoxical burning of a flame that does not hurt. Although up to this moment the "Canticle" had dealt with the experience of union only in terms of the spiritual marriage, the union is here indicated with the new symbol of the flame. Perhaps Saint John felt that the clumsy words of human passion were no longer sufficient to express the depth of his feeling. Perhaps the image of the flame only came to his mind accidentally here, after exhausting other traditional metaphorical language. It is possible that he completed the "Spiritual Canticle" when he had already written the "Living Flame of Love" and the image had crept from the later poem into the end of the earlier one. Or, perhaps, the "Living Flame of Love" burst in him as a consequence of a new stirring of his imagination produced by his own use of the word "flame" at the end of the "Canticle."

There is no way of knowing how the lines came to the poet, although we know that the image of the flame as a symbol of the union has been used traditionally in mystic writing as well as the symbol of the spiritual marriage. Neither one symbol nor the other nor the symbol of the night is new in the poetry of Saint John. His originality is to be found in the vigor of his expression and in the intonation of absolute sincerity of his language. One symbol can do as well as another to the true poet. As a matter of fact, there have been critics who have considered the use of the terms of human passion as a vulgar rendition of an experience high above the pleasures of the flesh. And yet, the skill of Saint John's verse has never been found to come short of perfection in rendering emotion and thought into the exact words necessary to evoke the mystery of his experience. When he turned towards the symbolic flame, it was indeed because he had reached the moment in which he had to write the final word of thankfulness for having completed the cycle of experience and expression.

In the structure of poetic crescendo that these three poems present, the last moment of rapture is expressed in the "Living Flame of Love." The four stanzas of this poem differ from the metrical serenity of the five-line stanzas of the preceding two. Now the stanza is longer, it has six lines, but it is clearly divided into two parts of three lines each linked by the rhyme. Each small section contains two short lines of seven syllables and one hendecasyllable. The longer third line, especially in the second part of the stanza, becomes the climactic synthesis of the exclamatory thought poured forth in the delight of the preceding lines:

> *¡Oh cauterio suave!*
> *¡Oh regalada llaga!*
> *¡Oh mano blanda! ¡Oh toque delicado,*
> *Que a vida eterna sabe,*
> *Y toda deuda paga!*
> *Matando, muerte en vida la has trocado.*

> (Oh gentle cautery!
> Oh delicate wound!
> Oh soft hand! Oh gentle touch
> That tastes of eternal life
> And repays every debt!
> By killing, death into life you have transformed!)

In this moment of extreme perplexity, there is no longer any need of words. In a few lines of rapturous thanksgiving, the poet praises this force that *delicadamente me enamoras* (delicately captures my love).

In no other verse of Saint John can we feel more deeply the exhilaration of the experience of living in a love that consumes all other thought and desire. The immense suffering of this undertaking and the immense joy it brings exact the ultimate and paradoxical request:

> *Acaba ya si quieres;*
> *Rompe la tela deste dulce encuentro.*
>
> (End finally, if you will,
> Break the web of this sweet meeting.)

The poetry of Saint John of the Cross comes to rest in these final lines that are both the testimony of an experience lived and the expression of a desire never to be fulfilled. A meeting that implores the end of the joy it brings becomes then the promise of an unattainable shore beyond pain and beyond happiness.

# CHAPTER 7

## The Lyrical Ecstasy

Apártalos, Amado,
Que voy de vuelo.
"Cántico espiritual"

(Look away, my Love,
For I am on the wing.
"Spiritual Canticle")

T HE hallucinatory darkness of a prison in Toledo gave Saint John the sounds of a few mysterious words. Through the years he built around them poems which conquered a world of listeners and which became his legacy to the future. In their turn, these poems gave origin to treatises of commentary and of theological inquiry. After a childhood of poverty and a full life of renunciation, Saint John's sufferings had been rewarded with the elusive freedom of a doctrine of spiritual perfection and a handful of exquisite rhymes. The subject of his poems and his meditations was the rapture of a moment in which his mind could transcend the limitations of the senses, the emotions, and even the shackles of reason itself. In a way unknown to anybody else he was able to transmute the ecstasy of his soul into ecstatic words.

When we read these poems today, every line renews the exalted feeling of discovery, every word recreates the joy of "sudden liberation" that is the mark of the successful image, "which presents an intellectual and emotional complex in an instant of time."[1] Ezra Pound adds to this description of the effect of a poetic image the assertion that writing an image in a lifetime is better than completing voluminous works. For Saint John it was compensation enough for all the tortures inflicted by an uncomprehending world and by his own determination to purify his soul.

On his deathbed, Saint John called for a recitation of his own poems sensing that in his lines he would hear our voices as we hear his in reading them again. Immortality breathed in his verses. He had known an experience of rapture that could only be repeated in the sounds of these words. We may never know for sure what it is like to transcend the limitations of the body, but the rapture of repeating Saint John's poems holds for us a revelation and a promise. The exhilaration of reading each one of his lines guides us towards the unattainable liberation of an experience beyond the reach of the imagination— an experience that somehow we have lived through during the moments of desiring and searching for it and which becomes a recollection before we know we have possessed it.

# Notes and References

## Chapter One

1. John Lynch, *Spain Under the Hapsburgs* (New York, 1964), I, 11.
2. John Huxtable Elliott, *Imperial Spain, 1469-1716* (London, 1963), p. 102.
3. "Cuando el hombre se desenfrena por la herejía . . . no es mucho que como caballo desbocado y sin freno juntamente pierda la obediencia a su rey." Padre Pedro de Rivadeneira, *Tratado del Príncipe Cristiano*, in *Obras escogidas del Padre de Rivadeneira* (Madrid, 1919), p. 500.
4. John Lynch, *op. cit.*, p. 213.
5. Henry Charles Lea, *A History of the Inquisition of Spain* (New York, 1922), III, 209.
6. John Lynch, *op. cit.*, p. 7.
7. Reginald Merton, *Cardinal Ximenes and the Making of Spain* (London, 1934), p. 66.
8. "Los sacerdotes debían residir, y debían también frecuentar la confesión lo más posible para celebrar con mayor pureza la misa. Los curas estaban obligados, bajo pena de multa, a explicar cada domingo a los fieles el evangelio del día y a enseñar la doctrina a los niños." Marcel Bataillon, *Erasmo y España* (Mexico, 1950), I, 3-4.
9. "El recogimiento no hace otra cosa sino vaciarnos de nosotros mesmos, para que Dios se extienda más en el corazón." Marcel Bataillon, *op. cit.*, p. 197.

## Chapter Two

1. John Lynch, *op. cit.*, p. 7.
2. Gabriela Cunninghame Graham, *Santa Teresa: Being Some Account of Her Life and Times* (London, 1894), I, 346.
3. E. W. Trueman Dicken, *The Crucible of Love* (New York, 1963), p. 36.
4. Rafael Altamira y Crevea, *A History of Spain. From the Beginnings to the Present Day*. Translated by Muna Lee (New York, 1949), p. 390.
5. Cristóbal Espejo y Julián Paz, *Las antiguas ferias de Medina del Campo* (Valladolid, 1912).

6. Claudio Sánchez-Albornoz, *España: un enigma histórico* (Buenos Aires, 1956), pp. 321, 324.

7. Jean Baruzi, *Saint Jean de la Croix et le problème de l'expérience mystique* (Paris, 1931), pp. 78-80.

## Chapter Three

1. Father Benedict Zimmerman, *Life of Saint John of the Cross* (London, 1927), p. 28.

2. "Il est indéniable, en tout cas, et ceci suffit à nous instruire, que ses ennemis voyaient en Jean de la Croix un être dangereux, dont on jugeait que l'influence n'était jamais assez conjurée." Jean Baruzi, *op. cit.*, p. 222.

## Chapter Four

1. Washington Irving, *The Alhambra* (Chicago, n. d.), pp. 45, 63-64.
2. Jean Baruzi, *op. cit.*, pp. 215-29.

## Chapter Five

1. David Lewis, *St. John of the Cross* (London, 1897), p. xxix.
2. Jean Vilnet, *La Biblia en la obra de San Juan de la Cruz* (Buenos Aires, 1953), p. 163.
3. Jean Baruzi, *op. cit.*, p. 137.
4. Leonard A. McCann, *The Doctrine of the Void* (Toronto, 1955), p. 31.
5. Rainier Maria Rilke, *The Book of Hours.* Translated by A. L. Peek (London, 1961), p. 114.
6. A Benedictine of Stanbrook Abbey, *Mediaeval Mystical Tradition and St. John of the Cross* (London, 1954), p. 61.
7. Bede Frost, *St. John of the Cross* (London, 1937), p. 162.
8. Edith Stein, *The Science of the Cross* (London, 1960), p. 181.

## Chapter Six

1. Dámaso Alonso, *La poesía de San Juan de la Cruz* (Madrid, 1942), p. 178.
2. The "Spiritual Canticle" is composed of thirty-nine stanzas, if we discount the doubtfully authentic eleventh stanza.
3. Dámaso Alonso, *op. cit.*, p. 186.

## Chapter Seven

1. *Literary Essays of Ezra Pound*, T. S. Eliot, ed. (London, 1954), p. 4.

# Selected Bibliography

1. Works of Saint John of the Cross

*Obras del místico doctor.* Edición critica y la más correcta y completa de las publicadas hasta hoy con introducciones y notas del padre Gerardo de San Juan de la Cruz (Toledo: Impr. Viuda e hijos de J. Paláez, 1912).

*El Cántico espiritual según el manuscrito de las Madres carmelitas de Jaén.* Edición y notas de Matías Martínez de Burgos (Madrid: Ediciones de "La Lectura," 1924).

*Poesías.* Recopilación y prólogo de Fr. Gerardo de San Juan de la Cruz (Madrid: B. del Amo, 1925).

*Cántico espiritual y poesías de San Juan de la Cruz, según el códice de Sanlúcar de Barrameda.* Edición y notas de P. Silverio de Santa Teresa, C. D. (Burgos: Tipografía "El Monte Carmelo," 1928).

*Poesías completas, Versos comentados, Avisos y sentencias, Cartas.* Edición, prólogo y notas de Pedro Salinas (Madrid: Signo, 1936).

*Poesías completas y otras páginas.* Selección, estudio y notas por Manuel Blecua (Zaragoza: Editorial Ebro, 1946).

*Vida y obras de San Juan de la Cruz, Doctor de la Iglesia Universal.* Biografía inédita del Santo por el R. P. Crisógono de Jesús, O.C.D. (Madrid: Biblioteca de Autores Cristianos, 1950).

*Poesías completas y comentarios en prosa a los poemas mayores.* Nota preliminar y edición de las poesías por Dámaso Alonso. Edición de los comentarios por Eulalia Galvarriato de Alonso (Madrid: Aguilar, 1963).

*Obras escogidas.* Edición y prólogo de Ignacio B. Anzoátegui (Madrid: Espasa-Calpe, 1964).

*Obras.* Introducción, prólogo y notas de José Luis L. Aranguren (Barcelona: Editorial Vergara, 1965).

2. Translations into English

*The Complete Works of Saint John of the Cross.* Translated from the original Spanish by D. Lewis. Edited by the Oblate Fathers of Saint Charles, with a Preface by Cardinal Wiseman (London, 1864), 2 vols. (2d ed., London: T. Baker, 1889.)

*The Dark Night of the Soul by Saint John of the Cross of the Order of Mount Carmel.* 4th ed., rev. Compared with the last critical Spanish edition of the works of the Saint of R. P. Gerardo de San Juan de la Cruz (London: T. Baker, 1916).

*The Ascent of Mount Carmel by St. John of the Cross.* Translated by David Lewis, with corrections and a prefatory essay on the development of mysticism in the Carmelite Order by Benedict Zimmerman, O.C.D. (London: T. Baker, 1922).

*The Dark Night of the Soul.* Introductory essay of Benedict Zimmerman (London: T. Baker, 1924).

*The Complete Works of Saint John of the Cross, Doctor of the Church.* Translated from the critical edition of P. Silverio de Santa Teresa, C.D., and edited by E. Allison Peers (London: Burns, Oates & Washbourne, Ltd., 1934-35).

*The Poems of St. John of the Cross.* The Spanish text with a translation by Roy Campbell (New York: Pantheon Books, 1951).

*The Dark Night of the Soul.* Edited, translated and abridged by Kurt F. Reinhardt (New York: F. Ungar Publishing Company, 1957).

*Poems.* Original Spanish texts and new English versions by John Frederick Nims (New York: Grove Press, 1959).

*Ascent of Mount Carmel.* 3d. rev. ed. Translated and edited with a general introduction by E. Allison Peers from the critical edition of P. Silverio de Santa Teresa (Garden City, New York: Image Books, 1962).

*The Collected Works of St. John of the Cross.* Translated by Kieran Kavanaugh and Otilio Rodríguez (New York: Doubleday, 1963).

*The Poems of Saint John of the Cross.* English versions and introduction by Willis Barnstone (Bloomington, Indiana: University of Indiana Press, 1968).

3. Studies on Saint John of the Cross

A BENEDICTINE OF STANBROOK ABBEY. *Mediaeval Mystical Tradition and Saint John of the Cross* (London: Burns & Oates, 1954).

ALONSO, DAMASO. *La poesía de San Juan de la Cruz* (Madrid: Consejo Superior de Investigaciones Científicas, 1942).

ASIN PALACIOS, MIGUEL. *Huellas del Islam. Sto. Tomás de Aquino. Turmeda. Pascal. S. Juan de la Cruz* (Madrid: Espasa-Calpe, s. a., 1941).

BARUZI, JEAN. *Saint Jean de la Croix et le problème de l'expérience mystique.* 2. éd., rev. et augm. (Paris: F. Alcan, 1931).

BRENAN, GERALD. "Saint John of the Cross, His Life and Poetry," in *Horizon*, XV, (1947), 256-81, 324-56.

BRUNO DE JESUS-MARIE. *Life of Saint John of the Cross.* English edition. Edited by Benedict Zimmerman. Introduction by Jacques Maritain (London: Sheed & Ward, 1932).

————. *San Juan de la Cruz* (Buenos Aires: Ediciones Desclée de Brouwer et Cie., 1944).

————. *Three Mystics: El Greco, St. John of the Cross, St. Teresa de Avila* (New York: Sheed & Ward, 1949).

————. *Vie d'amour de Saint Jean de la Croix* (Paris: Desclée de Brouwer et Cie., 1944).

CHANDEBOIS, HENRI. *Portrait de Saint Jean de la Croix* (Paris: Grasset, 1947).

CHEVALLIER, DOM, O.S.B. *Le Cantique Spirituel de Saint Jean de la Croix, Docteur de l'Eglise* (Belgium: Desclée de Brouwer & Cie., 1930).

————. "Le Cantique spirituel a-t-il été interpolé?" *Bulletin Hispanique*, 1922 (XXIV), 307-42.

CRISOGONO DE JESUS SACRAMENTADO. *San Juan de la Cruz: El hombre, el doctor, el poeta* (Barcelona: Editorial Labor, s. a., 1935).

————. *San Juan de la Cruz: su obra científica y su obra literaria* (Madrid: Editorial Mensajero de Sta. Teresa y San Juan de la Cruz, 1929).

————. *The Life of St. John of the Cross.* Translated by Kathleen Pond (New York: Harper, 1958).

————. *Vida y obras; biografía inédita del Santo* (Madrid: Biblioteca de autores cristianos, 1950).

CRISTIANI, LEON. *St. John of the Cross, Prince of Mystical Theology.* Translated from the French (New York: Doubleday, 1962).

DIAZ INFANTE NUNEZ, JOSEFINA. *La poesía de San Juan de la Cruz. Influencias y coincidencias* (Mexico: UNAM, 1956).

DICKEN, E. W. TRUEMAN. *The Crucible of Love; a Study of the Mysticism of St. Teresa of Jesus and St. John of the Cross* (New York: Sheed and Ward, 1963).

DOMINGUEZ BERRUETA, JUAN. *Vida y pensamiento de San Juan de la Cruz; un cántico a lo divino* (Barcelona: Editorial Araluce, n. d.).

ESCRITORES DEL SIGLO XVI. T. I. (Madrid: Biblioteca de Autores Españoles, 1853-55).

FRANCOIS DE SAINTE-MARIE, O.C.D. *Initiation à Saint Jean de la Croix* (Paris: [Coll. La Vigne du Carmel] Edit. du Seuil, 1945).

FROST, BEDE. *Saint John of the Cross, 1542-1591, Doctor of Divine Love; an Introduction to his Philosophy, Theology and Spirituality* (London: Hodder & Stoughton, 1937).

GARRIGOU-LAGRANGE, REGINALD. *Perfection chrétienne et contemplation selon S. Thomas d'Aquin et S. Jean de la Croix.* 4. éd. (Paris: Librairie Desclée et Cie., 1923).

GEORGE, ROBERT ESMONDE GORDON. *Carmelite and Poet, a Framed Portrait of St. John of the Cross, with his Poems in Spanish* by Robert Sencourt, pseud., (New York: The Macmillan Company, 1944).

GUILLEN, JORGE. "The Ineffable Language of Mysticism: San Juan de la Cruz," in *Language and Poetry* (Cambridge, Mass.: Harvard University Press, 1961).

HOORNAERT, RODOLPHE. *L'âme ardente de S. Jean de la Croix* (Tournai: Casterman, 1947).

ICAZA, ROSA MARIA. *The Stylistic Relationship Between Poetry and Prose in the Cántico espiritual of San Juan de la Cruz* (Washington: Catholic Universtiy of America Press, 1957).

KRYNEN, JEAN. *Le Cantique spirituel de saint Jean de la Croix commenté et refondu au XVIIe siècle; un regard sur l'histoire de l'exégèse du Cantique de Jaén* (Salamanca: Universidad de Salamanca, 1948).

LEWIS, DAVID. *Life of Saint John of the Cross* (London: T. Baker, 1897).

LUCIEN-MARIE DE SAINT-JOSEPH. *Poèmes mystiques de Saint Jean de la Croix, Docteur de l'Eglise* (Paris: Desclée de Brouwer et Cie., 1945).

McCANN, LEONARD A. *The Doctrine of the Void* (Toronto: Basilian Press, 1955).

McMAHON, JOHN JOSEPH. *The Divine Union in the Subida del Monte Carmelo and the Noche oscura of Saint John of the Cross* (Washington, D. C.: The Catholic University of America Press, 1941).

MENDEZ PLANCARTE, ALFONSO. *San Juan de la Cruz en Méjico* (Mexico: Fondo de Cultura Económica, 1959).

MENENDEZ Y PELAYO, MARCELINO. *La mística española*. Ed. y estudio preliminar de Pedro Sáinz Rodríguez (Madrid: A. Aguado, 1956).

MILNER, MAX. *Poésie et vie mystique chez Saint Jean de la Croix*. Préf. de Jean Baruzi (Paris: Editions du Seuil, 1951).

MOREL, GEORGES. *Le Sens de l'existence selon Saint Jean de la Croix* (Paris: Edit. Montaigne [Aubier], 1961).

OROZCO DIAZ, EMILIO. *Poesía y mística; introducción a la lírica de San Juan de la Cruz* (Madrid: Ediciones Guadarrama, 1959).

PEERS, E. ALLISON. *Handbook to the Life and Times of St. Teresa and St. John of the Cross* (London: William Clower & Sons, 1954).

————. *St. John of the Cross and Other Lectures and Addresses. 1920-1945* (London: Faber and Faber Ltd., 1946).

————. *Spirit of Flame; a Study of St. John of the Cross* (London: SCM Press, 1961).

————. *Studies of the Spanish Mystics*. Vols. 1-2 (New York: Macmillan Co., 1927).

RUANO, NAZARIO, O.C.D. *"Desnudez."* *Lo místico y lo literario en San Juan de la Cruz* (Mexico: Editorial Polis, 1961).

SETIEN DE JESUS MARIA, E. G. *Las raíces de la poesía sanjuanista y Dámaso Alonso* (Burgos: Editorial "El Monte Carmelo," 1950).

SISTERS OF NOTRE DAME, MOUNT PLEASANT, LIVERPOOL. *Life of Saint John of the Cross, Mystical Doctor.* With an introduction by Father Benedict Zimmerman, O.C.D. (London: T. Baker, 1927).

SOBRINO, JOSE ANTONIO DE. *Estudios sobre San Juan de la Cruz y nuevos textos de su obra* (Madrid: Consejo Superior de Investigaciones Científicas, 1950).

SPITZER, LEO. "Three Poems on Ecstasy (John Donne, Saint John of the Cross, Richard Wagner)," in *A Method of Interpreting Literature* (New York: Russell and Russell, 1967).

STEIN, EDITH. *The Science of the Cross; A Study of St. John of the Cross.* Edited by Dr. L. Gelber and Fr. Romaeus Leuven. Translated by Hilda Graef (London: Burns & Oates, 1960).

VALLEE, (M. R. P.), O. P. *Saint Jean de la Croix: sa vie, sa doctrine. Sermons prêchés les 22, 23, 24 novembre 1891 au Carmel de Caen* (Lille: Desclée de Brouwer et Cie., 1892).

VILNET, JEAN. *Bible et mystique chez Saint Jean de la Croix* (Bruges: Desclée de Brouwer, 1949).

————. *La Biblia en la obra de San Juan de la Cruz* (Buenos Aires: Desclée de Brouwer, 1953).

WAACH, HILDEGARD. *San Juan de la Cruz.* Trad. Alfonso M.ª de Santa Teresa (Madrid: Rialp, 1960).

ZIMMERMAN, FATHER BENEDICT, O.C.D. *Life of Saint John of the Cross* (London: T. Baker, 1927).

4. General Works

ALTAMIRA Y CREVEA, RAFAEL. *A History of Spain: From the Beginnings to the Present Day.* Translated by Muna Lee (New York: Van Nostrand Co., 1949).

BATAILLON, MARCEL. *Erasme et l'Espagne: Recherches sur l'histoire spirituelle du XVIe siècle* (Paris: E. Droz, 1937).

————. *Erasmo y España: estudios sobre la historia espiritual del siglo XVI.* Translated by Antonio Alatorre (Mexico: Fondo de Cultura Económica, 1950).

CHUDOBA, BOHDAN. *Spain and the Empire (1519-1643)* (Chicago: University of Chicago Press, 1952).

ELLIOTT, JOHN HUXTABLE. *Imperial Spain, 1469-1716* (London: Arnold, 1963).

ESPEJO, CRISTOBAL Y PAZ, JULIAN. *Las antiguas ferias de Medina del Campo* (Valladolid: "Impr. del Colegio Santiago," 1908. Date on cover 1912).

FLORISOONE, MICHEL. *Esthétique et Mystique. D'après Saint Thérèse d'Avila et St. Jean de la Croix* (Paris: [Coll. "La Vigne du Carmel."] Edit. du Seuil, 1956).

GELDER, HERMAN AREND ENNO VAN. *The Two Reformations in the 16th Century; a Study of the Religious Aspects and Consequences of Renaissance and Humanism* (The Hague: M. Nijhoff, 1961).

GRAHAM, GABRIELA CUNNINGHAME. *Santa Teresa: Being Some Account of Her Life and Times.* 2 vols. (London: Adam and Charles Black, 1894).

HATZFELD, HELMUT. *Estudios literarios sobre mística española* (Madrid: Editorial Gredos, 1955).

IRVING, WASHINGTON. *The Alhambra* (Chicago: Donohue, Henneberry & Co., n. d.).

LEA, HENRY CHARLES. *A History of the Inquisition of Spain.* 4 vols. (New York: The Macmillan Company, 1922).

LYNCH, JOHN. *Spain under the Hapsburgs,* vol. 1 (New York: Oxford University Press, 1964).

MASSIGNON, LOUIS. *L'expérience mystique et les modes de stylisation littéraire* (Paris: Plon, 1927).

MERTON, REGINALD. *Cardinal Ximenes and the Making of Spain* (London: Degan Paul, Trench, Trubner & Co., Ltd., 1934).

PEERS, EDGAR ALLISON. *Spanish Mysticism; a Preliminary Survey* (London: Methuen & Co. Ltd., 1924).

POUND, EZRA. *Literary Essays of Ezra Pound* Edited by T. S. Eliot (London: James Laughlin, 1954).

RILKE, RAINIER MARIA. *The Book of Hours.* Translated by A. L. Peek (London: Hogarth Press, 1961).

RIVADENEIRA, PADRE PEDRO DE. *Tratado del Príncipe Cristiano,* in *Obras escogidas del Padre Pedro de Rivadeneira* (Madrid: Biblioteca de Autores Españoles, LX, 1919).

SAINZ Y RODRIGUEZ, PEDRO. *Introducción a la historia de la literatura mística en España* (Madrid: Editorial Voluntad, s. a., 1927).

SANCHEZ-ALBORNOZ, CLAUDIO. *España: un enigma histórico.* 2 vols. (Buenos Aires: Editorial Sudamericana, 1956).

# Poems of Saint John of The Cross

NOTE:

With the exception of nine *romances* or ballads, the translation of "Super flumina Babylonis," a couple of quatrains without artistic value, and a few poems of doubtful authenticity, the following pages contain most of the poetry of Saint John in Spanish accompanied by an almost literal translation. I hope that this translation will enable the reader to understand the forcefulness of the original better than an attempt at a poetic version, which would be doomed to failure precisely because of the extraordinary beauty of this poetry.

I. *Noche oscura del alma (Subida del Monte Carmelo)*
*Canciones del alma que se goza de haber llegado al alto estado*
*de la perfección, que es la unión con Dios, por el camino de la*
*negación spiritual.*

En una noche oscura,
Con ansias en amores inflamada,
¡Oh dichosa ventura!
Salí sin ser notada,
Estando ya mi casa sosegada.

A escuras, y segura,
Por la secreta escala disfrazada,
¡Oh dichosa ventura!
A escuras, y en celada,
Estando ya mi casa sosegada.

En la noche dichosa,
En secreto, que nadie me veía,
Ni yo miraba cosa,
Sin otra luz y guía
Sino la que en el corazón ardía.

Aquésta me guiaba
Más cierto que la luz del mediodía,
A donde me esperaba
Quien yo bien me sabía,
En parte donde nadie parecía.

¡Oh noche, que guiaste,
Oh noche amable más que el alborada!
¡Oh noche, que juntaste
Amado con amada,
Amada en el Amado transformada!

En mi pecho florido,
Que entero para él sólo se guardaba,
Allí quedó dormido,
Y yo le regalaba,
Y el ventalle de cedros aire daba.

## I. *Dark Night of the Soul (Ascent of Mount Carmel)*

Songs of the soul that rejoices in having arrived at the high state of perfection, which is union with God, by way of spiritual negation.

In the darkness of the night,
With love and longing seized,
Oh delightful happiness!
I went abroad unnoticed,
All then being quiet in my house.

In safety, in the dark,
Disguised, by the secret staircase,
Oh delightful happiness!
In the dark, stealthily,
All then being quiet in my house.

In the happiness of the night,
Secretly, unseen by anybody,
Looking at nothing else,
With no other light or guide
Save that which was burning in my heart.

This light guided me
More certain than the light of midday,
To where one awaited me
Whom I knew well
In a place where no one would appear.

Oh night that was my guide,
Oh night dearer than the dawn!
Oh night, that joined
Lover to beloved,
Transforming the bride into the Lover!

On my flowering breast,
That was saved only for him,
There he fell asleep,
And I caressed him,
And a fan of cedar trees waved the air.

*El aire de la almena,*
*Cuando yo sus cabellos esparcía,*
*Con su mano serena*
*En mi cuello hería,*
*Y todos mis sentidos suspendía.*

*Quedéme, y olvidéme,*
*El rostro recliné sobre el Amado,*
*Cesó todo, y dejéme,*
*Dejando mi cuidado*
*Entre las azucenas olvidado.*

## II. *Cántico espiritual*

*Canciones entre el alma y el Esposo.*

### ESPOSA

*¿A dónde te escondiste,*
*Amado, y me dejaste con gemido?*
*Como el ciervo huiste,*
*Habiéndome herido;*
*Salí tras ti clamando, y eras ido.*

*Pastores los que fuerdes*
*Allá por las majadas al otero,*
*Si por ventura vierdes*
*Aquel que yo más quiero,*
*Decidle que adolezco, peno y muero.*

*Buscando mis amores,*
*Iré por esos montes y riberas,*
*Ni cogeré las flores,*
*Ni temeré las fieras,*
*Y pasaré los fuertes y fronteras.*

### PREGUNTA A LAS CRIATURAS

*Oh bosques y espesuras,*
*Plantadas por la mano del Amado,*
*Oh prado de verduras,*
*De flores esmaltado,*
*Decid si por vosotros ha pasado.*

The breeze from the ramparts,
When I was playing with his hair,
With its serene hand
My neck wounded,
And suspended every one of my senses.

I stayed, lost to myself,
My face upon my lover I laid,
All endeavor ceased, I forgot myself,
And all my cares were left
Forgotten among the lilies.

## II. *Spiritual Canticle*

Songs between the soul and the Bridegroom.

### BRIDE

Where are you hiding,
Beloved, having left me to moan?
Like the stag you fled
After wounding me;
I followed crying aloud, but you had gone.

Shepherds, you that go
Through the sheepfolds to the hills,
If by chance you see
Him that I love most,
Tell him that I suffer, grieve, and die.

Searching for my love
I will wander amongst mountains and rivers,
I will not gather flowers
Nor fear the prowling beasts,
And I will pass through all the forts and frontiers.

### QUESTIONS TO THE CREATURES

Oh forests and thickets,
Sowed by the hand of the Beloved,
Oh meadow of green,
Spangled with blossoms,
Tell me if he has passed across you.

### RESPUESTA DE LAS CRIATURAS
Mil gracias derramando,
Pasó por estos sotos con presura,
Y, yéndolos mirando,
Con sola su figura
Vestidos los dejó de hermosura.


### ESPOSA
¡Ay, quién podrá sanarme!
Acaba de entregarte ya de vero,
No quieras enviarme
De hoy ya más mensajero,
Que no saben decirme lo que quiero.


Y todos cuantos vagan,
De ti me van mil gracias refiriendo
Y todos más me llagan,
Y déjame muriendo
Un no sé qué que quedan balbuciendo.


Mas ¿cómo perseveras,
Oh vida no viviendo donde vives,
Y haciendo porque mueras
Las flechas que recibes,
De lo que del Amado en ti concibes?


¿Por qué, pues has llagado
A aqueste corazón, no le sanaste?
Y pues me le has robado,
¿Por qué así le dejaste,
Y no tomas el robo que robaste?


Apaga mis enojos,
Pues que ninguno basta a deshacellos,
Y véante mis ojos,
Pues eres lumbre de ellos,
Y sólo para ti quiero tenellos.


Descubre tu presencia
Y máteme tu vista y hermosura:
Mira que la dolencia
De amor, que no se cura
Sino con la presencia y la figura.

### ANSWER OF THE CREATURES

Showering a thousand graces,
In haste he passed through these groves,
And, as he looked on them,
By the mere sight of his face
He clothed them in beauty.

### BRIDE

Alas, who can console my grief!
Make the last surrender in full truth,
Do not send me
Messengers any longer
Who cannot tell me what I desire.

All those around here,
Speak and recount your charms a thousand times
And each deals a deeper wound,
And they leave me dying in desire
Of that something they leave half said.

But, how can you go on,
Oh life, not living where you dwell,
And if the arrows you receive
From your Lover, as you imagine him
In yourself, are working towards your death?

Why, since you pierced
This heart, have you not healed it?
And since you have stolen it,
Why do you leave it
And do not take the plunder of your theft?

End my torments
Since no one else can still my sorrows,
And let my eyes see you,
Since you are their light
And my sight I have only to see you.

Reveal your presence,
And kill me with your beauty and with your eyes:
Remember that the suffering
Of love can only be cured
With the presence of the face loved.*

*This stanza is not found in some redactions of the "Cántico espiritual," and its authenticity is questionable.

*¡Oh cristalina fuente,*
*Si en esos tus semblantes plateados,*
*Formases de repente*
*Los ojos deseados*
*Que tengo en mis entrañas dibujados!*


*Apártalos, Amado,*
*Que voy de vuelo.*


### ESPOSO

*Vuélvete, paloma,*
*Que el ciervo vulnerado*
*Por el otero asoma,*
*Al aire de tu vuelo, y fresco toma.*


### ESPOSA

*Mi Amado, las montañas,*
*Los valles solitarios, nemorosos,*
*Las ínsulas extrañas,*
*Los ríos sonorosos,*
*El silbo de los aires amorosos.*


*La noche sosegada*
*En par de los levantes de la aurora,*
*La música callada,*
*La soledad sonora,*
*La cena, que recrea y enamora.*


*Nuestro lecho florido*
*De cuevas de leones enlazado,*
*En púrpura tendido,*
*De paz edificado,*
*De mil escudos de oro coronado.*


*A zaga de tu huella*
*Las jóvenes discurren el camino*
*Al toque de centella,*
*Al adobado vino,*
*Emisiones de bálsamo divino.*

Oh crystalline spring,
If only in your silver surface,
You could make suddenly appear
The eyes for which I long
And which are graven in my innermost heart!


Look away, my Love,
For I am on the wing.


### THE BRIDEGROOM
Turn back, dove,
The wounded hart
On the hill appears,
Refreshed by the wind of your flight.


### BRIDE
My Love, the mountain range,
The solitary melancholy valleys,
The islands far and strange,
The pleasant sounding rivers,
The whistling of loving breezes.


The quiet night
Just before the coming of dawn,
The silent music,
The musical solitude,
The supper that entertains and enamours.


Our bed with flowers,
With dens of lions around it,
Spread in purple,
Built in peace,
Crowned by a thousand shields of gold.


Following your footprint
The maidens roam the roadways
Having touched the spark,
Tasted the spiced wine,
Emanated from a divine balm.

En la interior bodega
De mi amado bebí, y cuando salía
Por toda aquesta vega,
Ya cosa no sabía,
Y el ganado perdí, que antes seguía.

Allí me dio su pecho,
Allí me enseñó ciencia muy sabrosa,
Y yo le di de hecho
A mí, sin dejar cosa;
Allí le prometí de ser su esposa.

Mi alma se ha empleado,
Y todo mi caudal en su servicio:
Ya no guardo ganado,
Ni ya tengo otro oficio;
Que ya sólo en amar es mi ejercicio.

Pues ya si en el ejido,
De hoy más no fuere vista ni hallada,
Diréis que me he perdido,
Que andando enamorada,
Me hice perdidiza, y fui ganada.

De flores y esmeraldas
En las frescas mañanas escogidas,
Haremos las guirnaldas,
En tu amor florecidas
Y en un cabello mío entretejidas.

En solo aquel cabello
Que en mi cuello volar consideraste,
Mirástele en mi cuello,
Y en él preso quedaste,
Y en uno de mis ojos te llagaste.

Cuando tú me mirabas,
Tu gracia en mí tus ojos imprimían;
Por eso me adamabas,
Y en eso merecían
Los míos adorar lo que en ti vían.

No quieras despreciarme,
Que si color moreno en mí hallaste,
Ya bien puedes mirarme,
Después que me miraste,
Que gracia y hermosura en mí dejaste.

In the deep cellar
Of my beloved I drank, and I wandered
In this meadow,
Having forgotten everything;
And I lost the flock I used to follow.

There he gave me his breast,
There he taught me the sweetest science,
And I gave him truly
All of me, keeping nothing back;
There I promised him to be his bride.

My soul is in his service
And all my riches too,
Flocks I no longer keep
Nor any other work I have,
My only duty now is to love.

So now, if in the common lands
I am no longer found or seen,
Say that I went astray,
That being in love,
I was lost, and I was found again.

Of flowers and emeralds
Gathered in the cool mornings,
We will garlands make,
Blooming with your love
And twine around one hair of mine.

In that one hair
That you watched fluttering on my neck,
You looked at it on my neck,
And you were made a captive
And you were wounded by one of my eyes.

When you were looking at me,
Your grace upon me your eyes imprinted,
That was the reason for your love,
And that is why my eyes
Deserved to love what they saw in yours.

Do not scorn me,
Although you found me to be dark,
You may now look at me,
Since after you saw me
You have endowed me with grace and beauty.

Cazadnos las raposas,
Que está ya florecida nuestra viña,
En tanto que de rosas
Hacemos una piña,
Y no parezca nadie en la montiña.

Detente, cierzo muerto;
Ven, Austro, que recuerdas los amores,
Aspira por mi huerto,
Y corran tus olores,
Y pacerá el Amado entre las flores.

### ESPOSO

Entrádose ha la Esposa
En el ameno huerto deseado,
Y a su sabor reposa,
El cuello reclinado
Sobre los dulces brazos del Amado.

Debajo del manzano,
Allí conmigo fuiste desposada,
Allí te di la mano,
Y fuiste reparada,
Donde tu madre fuera violada.

A las aves ligeras,
Leones, ciervos, gamos saltadores,
Montes, valles, riberas,
Aguas, aires, ardores,
Y miedos de las noches veladores:

Por las amenas liras
Y canto de sirenas os conjuro
Que cesen vuestras iras,
Y no toquéis al muro,
Porque la Esposa duerma más seguro.

### ESPOSA

Oh ninfas de Judea,
En tanto que en las flores y rosales
El ámbar perfumea,
Morá en los arrabales,
Y no queráis tocar nuestros umbrales.

Hunt out the foxes,
For our vine is already in full flower,
While a bundle
We make of roses,
And let no one come near the hillside.

Cease, Northern gale;
Come, Southern breeze, recalling love,
Breathe in my orchard,
Pervaded by sweet scents,
And the Beloved will tarry among the flowers.

### BRIDEGROOM

The Bride has entered
The longed-for orchard of delights,
And she rests at her ease,
Her neck leaning
Against the gentle arms of the Beloved.

Beneath the apple tree,
There you were betrothed to me,
There I pledged my hand to you,
In reparation
Where your mother had been violated.

You swift birds,
Lions, stags, and leaping roebucks,
Forests, valleys, shores,
Springs, winds, heat of summer,
And fears that wake the night:

By the pleasant lyres
And the sirens' sweet song, I conjure you
To cease in all your tumults,
And do not rap on the wall,
So that the Bride may sleep in peace.

### BRIDE

Oh nymphs of Judaea,
While yet amber perfume invades
The flowers and rose bushes,
Keep away in the outskirts,
And do not come across our threshold.

*Escóndete, Carillo,*
*Y mira con tu haz a las montañas,*
*Y no quieras decillo;*
*Mas mira las compañas*
*De la que va por ínsulas extrañas.*

### ESPOSO

*La blanca palomica*
*Al arca con el ramo se ha tornado,*
*Y ya la tortolica*
*Al socio deseado*
*En las riberas verdes ha hallado.*

*En soledad vivía,*
*Y en soledad ha puesto ya su nido,*
*Y en soledad la guía*
*A solas su querido,*
*También en soledad de amor herido.*

### ESPOSA

*Gocémonos, Amado,*
*Y vámonos a ver en tu hermosura,*
*Al monte y al collado,*
*Do mana el agua pura;*
*Entremos más adentro en la espesura.*

*Y luego a las subidas*
*Cavernas de la piedra nos iremos,*
*Que están bien escondidas,*
*Y allí nos entraremos,*
*Y el mosto de granadas gustaremos.*

*Allí me mostrarías*
*Aquello que mi alma pretendía,*
*Y luego me darías*
*Allí, tú, vida mía*
*Aquello que me diste el otro día.*

*El aspirar del aire,*
*El canto de la dulce filomena,*
*El soto y su donaire,*
*En la noche serena,*
*Con llama que consume y no da pena.*

Hide, my darling,
And look with your eyes on the mountains,
And do not dare to speak;
But watch the retinue
Of her who sails among the strange islands.

### BRIDEGROOM

The little white dove
Has returned to the ark with her branch,
And the turtle dove
Her desired mate
Has found on the green banks of the river.

In solitude she lived,
And in solitude she has built her nest,
In solitude she is guided
By her solitary lover,
Also in solitude wounded by love.

### BRIDE

Let us rejoice, my Love,
And let us go to see your beauty,
Upon the mountain or in the meadow,
Where pure water springs,
Let us go deeper into the forest.

And then to the very high
And rocky caverns we will go,
Which are well hidden,
And there we will enter,
And we will taste of the wine of pomegranates.

Up there you will show me
What my soul has longed for,
And then you will give me
There, my love,
The same gift you gave long ago.

The softness of the air,
The sweet song of Philomel,
The charm of the grove,
In the quiet of the night
With fire that consumes without hurting.

Que nadie lo miraba,
Aminadab tampoco parecía,
Y el cerco sosegaba,
Y la caballería
A vista de las aguas descendía.

III.  Llama de amor viva

Canciones del alma en la íntima comunicación de unión de amor
de Dios.

¡Oh llama de amor viva,
Qué tiernamente hieres
De mi alma en el más profundo centro!
Pues ya no eres esquiva,
Acaba ya si quieres;
Rompe la tela deste dulce encuentro!

¡Oh cauterio suave!
¡Oh regalada llaga!
¡Oh mano blanda! ¡Oh toque delicado,
Que a vida eterna sabe
Y toda deuda paga!
Matando, muerte en vida la has trocado.

¡Oh lámparas de fuego,
En cuyos resplandores
Las profundas cavernas del sentido,
Que estaba oscuro y ciego,
Con extraños primores
Calor y luz dan junto a su querido!

¡Cuán manso y amoroso
Recuerdas en mi seno,
Donde secretamente solos moras!
Y en tu aspirar sabroso,
De bien y gloria lleno,
¡Cuán delicadamente me enamoras!

IV.  Coplas hechas sobre un éxtasis de alta contemplación.

Entréme donde no supe,
Y quedéme no sabiendo,
Toda sciencia trascendiendo.

> And no creature could see it,
> Neither could Aminadab appear,
> And the siege was quieted,
> And the horsemen
> Dismounted to look on the waters.

### III. *Living Flame of Love*

Songs of the soul in the intimate communication of union in the love of God.

> Oh living flame of love,
> How tenderly you wound
> The innermost center of my soul!
> Since you are no longer fleeing,
> End finally, if you will,
> Break the web of this sweet meeting.

> Oh gentle cautery!
> Oh delicate wound!
> Oh soft hand! Oh gentle touch
> That tastes of eternal life
> And repays every debt!
> By killing, death into life you have transformed!

> Oh lamps of fire,
> In whose resplendent light
> The deep caverns of the senses
> That were dark and blind
> With strange new beauty
> Give warmth and light to their beloved!

> How tender and loving
> You awaken in my breast,
> Where in secret alone you dwell:
> In your delicate breathing
> Full of grace and glory,
> How delicately you capture my love!

### IV. *Songs written about an ecstasy of high contemplation.*

> I entered I knew not where
> And I remained, knowing nothing, where
> All science was transcended.

Yo no supe dónde entraba,
Pero, cuando allí me vi,
Sin saber dónde me estaba,
Grandes cosas entendí;
No diré lo que sentí,
Que me quedé no sabiendo,
Toda sciencia trascendiendo.

De paz y de piedad
Era la sciencia perfecta,
En profunda soledad,
Entendida vía recta;
Era cosa tan secreta,
Que me quedé balbuciendo,
Toda sciencia trascendiendo.

Estaba tan embebido,
Tan absorto y ajenado,
Que se quedó mi sentido
De todo sentir privado;
Y el espíritu dotado
De un entender no entendiendo,
Toda sciencia trascendiendo.

El que allí llega de vero,
De sí mismo desfallesce;
Cuanto sabía primero.
Mucho bajo le paresce;
Y su sciencia tanto cresce,
Que se queda no sabiendo,
Toda sciencia trascendiendo.

Cuanto más alto se sube,
Tanto menos entendía
Que es la tenebrosa nube
Que a la noche esclarecía;
Por eso quien la sabía
Queda siempre no sabiendo
Toda sciencia trascendiendo.

I did not know where I was entering
But when I found myself there,
Not knowing where I was,
I understood hidden things;
I cannot say what I felt,
Since I remained knowing nothing, where
All science was transcended.


Of peace and compassion
The perfect science was made,
In profound solitude
The straight way was clear;
It was so secret a way
That I could only stammer, where
All science was transcended.


I was so engrossed,
So absorbed and swept away,
That my senses were deprived
Of all manner of sensing;
And my spirit was endowed
With an unknowing knowledge, where
All science was transcended.


Whoever truly to this place has come
Begins to lose consciousness;
All he thought he knew before
Seems to him to be worthless;
And his knowledge increases so much
That he remains knowing nothing, where
All science was transcended.


The higher one climbs
The less one understands
Since it is the darkest cloud
That gives light to the darkness of the night;
And so whoever knows this
Remains always knowing nothing, where
All science was transcended.

Este saber no sabiendo
Es de tan alto poder,
Que los sabios arguyendo
Jamás le pueden vencer;
Que no llega su saber
A no entender entendiendo,
Toda sciencia trascendiendo.

Y es de tan alta excelencia
Aqueste sumo saber,
Que no hay facultad ni sciencia
Que le puedan emprender;
Quien se supiere vencer
Con un no saber sabiendo,
Irá siempre trascendiendo.

Y si lo queréis oir,
Consiste esta suma sciencia
En un subido sentir
De la divinal Esencia;
Es obra de su clemencia
Hacer quedar no entendiendo,
Toda sciencia trascendiendo.

V.   Coplas del alma que pena por ver a Dios.

Vivo sin vivir en mí,
Y de tal manera espero,
Que muero porque no muero.

En mí yo no vivo ya,
Y sin Dios vivir no puedo;
Pues sin él y sin mí quedo,
Este vivir ¿qué será?
Mil muertes se me hará,
Pues mi misma vida espero,
Muriendo porque no muero.

Esta vida que yo vivo
Es privación de vivir;
Y así, es contino morir
Hasta que viva contigo;
Oye, mi Dios, lo que digo,
Que esta vida no la quiero;
Que muero porque no muero.

This unknowing knowledge
Is of so strong a force
That wise men in their disputations
Can never defeat it:
Since their wisdom never reaches
The unknowing understanding, where
All science is transcended.

And it is so high in its virtue
This highest of all knowledge;
That there is no school or science
That can undertake to know it;
Whoever knows how to defeat himself
With an unknowing knowledge.
Will always be transcending science.

And if you want to hear:
This highest of all science
Consists in a deep and high feeling
Of the divine Essence;
It is the work of His mercy
That makes one remain unknowing, where
All science is transcended.

V. *Songs of the soul that pines to see God.*

I live, but yet I do not live
In me. My hopes fly so high that
I die because I do not die.

I do not live in myself,
And without God I cannot live;
Since I am left without Him and without me,
This living, what will it be for?
It will be like a thousand deaths,
Since my true life I am hoping for,
Dying because I do not die.

This life I lead is only
A way of not living, that is,
It will be a constant death
Until I live in you.
Listen, my God, to what I say:
This life I do not want, for
I die because I do not die.

Estando absente de ti,
¿Qué vida puedo tener,
Sino muerte padescer,
La mayor que nunca vi?
Lástima tengo de mí,
Pues de suerte persevero,
Que muero porque no muero.


El pez que del agua sale,
Aun de alivio no caresce,
Que en la muerte que padesce,
Al fin la muerte le vale;
¿Qué muerte habrá que se iguale
A mi vivir lastimero,
Pues si más vivo más muero?


Cuando me pienso aliviar
De verte en el Sacramento,
Háceme más sentimiento
El no te poder gozar;
Todo es para más penar,
Por no verte como quiero,
Y muero porque no muero.


Y si me gozo, Señor,
Con esperanza de verte,
En ver que puedo perderte
Se me dobla mi dolor:
Viviendo en tanto pavor,
Y esperando como espero,
Muérome porque no muero.


Sácame de aquesta muerte,
Mi Dios, y dame la vida;
No me tengas impedida
En este lazo tan fuerte;
Mira que peno por verte,
Y mi mal es tan entero,
Que muero porque no muero.

Being absent from You,
What life can I have,
Save this suffering of death,
The greatest death I ever saw?
Great pity I have for myself,
Because I persevere in such fashion that
I die because I do not die.


The fish that leaves the water
Does not lack consolation,
For the death he suffers
Is a final death to him:
What death can there be to compare
To this miserable life,
Since the more I live the more I die?


When I seek consolation
Looking at You in the Sacrament,
It increases my suffering
Not to be able to enjoy You;
Everything adds to my grief,
For not seeing You as I wish
I die because I do not die.


I rejoice, my Lord,
In the hope of seeing You,
But seeing how I may lose You,
My grief is then doubled.
Living in such terror,
And hoping as I hope,
I die because I do not die.


Rescue me from this death,
My God, and give me life,
Do not bind me
In such strong bonds:
See that I pine to see You,
And my grief is so complete that
I die because I do not die.

Lloraré mi muerte ya,
Y lamentaré mi vida
En tanto que detenida
Por mis pecados está.
¡Oh mi Dios! ¿cuándo será?
Cuando yo diga de vero:
Vivo ya porque no muero.

VI.    Otras a lo divino.

Tras de un amoroso lance,
Y no de esperanza falto,
Volé tan alto, tan alto,
Que le di a la caza alcance.

Para que yo alcance diese
A aqueste lance divino,
Tanto volar me convino,
Que de vista me perdiese;
Y con todo, en este trance
En el vuelo quedé falto;
Mas el amor fue tan alto,
Que le di a la caza alcance.

Cuando más alto subía,
Deslumbróseme la vista,
Y la más fuerte conquista
En escuro se hacía;
Mas por ser de amor el lance
Di un ciego y oscuro salto,
Y fui, tan alto, tan alto,
Que le di a la caza alcance.

Cuanto más alto llegaba
De este lance tan subido,
Tanto más bajo y rendido
Y abatido me hallaba;
Dije: No habrá quien alcance;
Y abatíme tanto, tanto,
Que fui tan alto, tan alto,
Que le di a la caza alcance.

I will mourn my death,
And lament my life now,
Since it is prolonged
Because of all my sins,
Oh, my God! When will it be
That I will be able to say:
I live because I do not die?


VI.   *Other songs with a divine meaning.*


In the quest of love
—Not without hope, of course—
I soared so high, so high,
That I was able to catch my prey.


So that I could catch my prey
In this quest divine,
I needed to fly so high
That I was lost sight of;
Even so, in this adventure
My flight fell short of its goal;
Yet love could soar so high
That I was able to catch my prey.


As I was soaring higher
My eyes were dazzled
And the greatest conquest ever
Was conquered in the dark:
But since it was a quest of love
I jumped blindly in the dark,
And soared so high, so high
That I was able to catch my prey.


And the higher I reached
In this quest of height
The lower and more base I felt
In great dejection;
I said: nobody can reach that prey,
And so dejected did I feel
That I soared so high, so high
That I was able to catch my prey.

Por una extraña manera
Mil vuelos pasé de un vuelo,
Porque esperanza de cielo
Tanto alcanza cuanto espera;
Esperé sólo este lance,
Y en esperar no fui falto,
Pues fui tan alto, tan alto,
Que le di a la caza alcance.

VII.    Otras canciones a lo divino de Cristo y el alma.

Un pastorcico solo está penado,
Ajeno de placer y de contento,
Y en su pastora puesto el pensamiento,
Y el pecho del amor muy lastimado.

No llora por haberle amor llagado,
Que no le pena verse así afligido,
Aunque en el corazón está herido;
Mas llora por pensar que está olvidado.

Que sólo de pensar que está olvidado
De su bella pastora, con gran pena
Se deja maltratar en tierra ajena,
El pecho del amor muy lastimado.

Y dice el Pastorcico: ¡Ay, desdichado
De aquel que de mi amor ha hecho ausencia,
Y no quiere gozar la mi presencia,
Y el pecho por su amor muy lastimado!

Y a cabo de un gran rato se ha encumbrado
Sobre un árbol do abrió sus brazos bellos,
Y muerto se ha quedado, asido de ellos,
El pecho del amor muy lastimado.

VIII.   Cantar del alma que se huelga de conoscer a Dios por fe.

Que bien sé yo la fonte que mana y corre,
Aunque es de noche.

Aquella eterna fonte está ascondida,
Que bien sé yo do tiene su manida,
Aunque es de noche.

In the strangest of all ways
A thousand flights I flew in one,
Because the hope of heaven
Reaches everything it hopes for;
It was adventure of hope only
And my hope was so profound
That I soared so high, so high,
That I was able to catch my prey.

VII.   *Other songs in the same divine manner between Christ and the soul.*

A shepherd in loneliness is grieving,
Far from pleasure and contentment,
His thoughts dwelling on his shepherdess,
And his breast of love sorely wounded.

He does not cry for love that hurts,
Since he does not grieve for being with love afflicted,
Although he is wounded in his heart,
But he cries because he thinks he is forgotten.

Just because he thinks he has been forgotten
By his beautiful shepherdess, with great sorrow
He allows others to maltreat him in a strange land,
His breast of love sorely wounded.

And the shepherd says: alas, woe to the one
Who has transformed my love into forgetfulness,
And does not desire the joy of my presence,
And my breast of her love sorely wounded!

And after a long while he climbed
A tree and opened his wide arms,
And dead he remains there, bound by his arms,
His breast of love sorely wounded.

VIII.   *Song of the soul that rejoices in knowing God through faith.*

Well I know the fountain that flows and runs
Although it's night.

That eternal fountain is well hidden,
And well I know where its source is,
Although it's night.

Su origen no lo sé, pues no le tiene,
Mas sé que todo origen de ella viene,
Aunque es de noche.

Sé que no puede ser cosa tan bella,
Y que cielos y tierra beben de ella,
Aunque es de noche.

Bien sé que suelo en ella no se halla,
Y que ninguno puede vadealla,
Aunque es de noche.

Su claridad nunca es escurecida,
Y sé que toda luz de ella es venida,
Aunque es de noche.

Sé ser tan caudalosas sus corrientes,
Que infiernos, cielos riegan, y las gentes,
Aunque es de noche.

El corriente que nace de esta fuente,
Bien sé que es tan capaz y omnipotente,
Aunque es de noche.

El corriente que de estas dos procede
Sé que ninguna de ellas le precede,
Aunque es de noche.

Aquesta eterna fonte está escondida
En este vivo pan por darnos vida,
Aunque es de noche.

Aquí se está llamando a las criaturas,
Y de esta agua se hartan, aunque a escuras,
Porque es de noche.

Aquesta viva fuente, que deseo,
En este pan de vida yo la veo,
Aunque de noche.

I do not know its origin, for it has none,
But I do know that everything in it has its beginning,
Although it's night.

I know there cannot be a thing of such beauty,
And that heavens and earth drink there,
Although it's night.

Well I know that there is no bottom to it,
And that nobody can wade through it,
Although it's night.

I know her clarity can never be obscured,
And that all light comes from it,
Although it's night.

I know her streams carry so much water
That they water the inferno, and heaven, and all peoples,
Although it's night.

The stream that is born from this fountain
Well I know is omnipotent in its force,
Although it's night.

The stream that comes from these two sources,
Is not preceded by either of them,
Although it's night.

This eternal spring is hidden
In this live bread to give us life,
Although it's night.

Here it calls all creatures forth
And this water satisfies them, although it's dark
Because it's night.

This living fountain that I so much desire,
In this bread of life I can see,
Even at night.

# Index